FRIGHTWRITE

Beware, Your Wish Could Come True

FrightWrite

A GHASTLY GOOD Reading and Writing Program

Beware, Your Wish Could Come True

JAMESTOWN PUBLISHERS

a division of NTC/Contemporary Publishing Group
Lincolnwood, Illinois USA

Editorial Director: Cynthia Krejcsi

Executive Editor: Marilyn Cunningham

Editorial Services Manager: Sylvia Bace

Market Development Manager: Mary Sue Dillingofski

Design Manager: Ophelia M. Chambliss

Production and Design: PiperStudiosInc

Cover Composition: Doug Besser

Production Manager: Margo Goia

ISBN: 0-89061-863-1

Published by Jamestown Publishers,
a division of NTC/Contemporary Publishing Group, Inc.,
4255 West Touhy Avenue,
Lincolnwood (Chicago), Illinois 60646-1975 U.S.A.
© 1997 by NTC/Contemporary Publishing Group, Inc.

9 0 1 2 3 4 VL 8 7 6 5 4 3 2

CONTENTS

To the Reader

BE WARNED!

Be warned—the stories in this book could make your blood run cold. They could also give you nightmares and make your flesh crawl. You might even wish that you had never picked up the book. On second thought, wishing is a bad idea. Who knows what could happen!

Actually, the stories in this book could make one of your wishes come true—your wish to become a ghastly good writer. See how professional writers lay out a grisly plot and visualize a story. Find out how to show terror instead of tell about it. Learn how to write dark stories that will send chills up your reader's spine.

Learn how to **FRIGHTWRITE!**

What Goes Around Comes Around

"What goes around comes around," Dillon had said just before he died. Jennifer bit her lip at the memory. His funeral had been last November, four months ago, but his words still came back to haunt her.

She knew that what she had done was wrong, but she'd wanted so badly to win the competition. She *had* to win.

It had all started innocently enough, in the computer lab at school. . . .

Jennifer's laptop computer was in for repairs. The deadline for the writing contest was the next day, so she went to the computer lab to put the finishing touches on her entry.

There was already a disk in the <u>drive</u> of the computer she chose, but the screen had gone back to the main menu. She reached to exchange the disk for her own but, on a sudden impulse, decided to sneak a peek at what was on the disk instead.

A story came up on the screen. It was about a boy from a poor neighborhood. He was a member of a motorcycle gang, and his secret ambition was to write. From the moment she began to read, Jennifer knew the story would

drive: a part of a computer that reads the information stored on disks

win the contest. It was real life, written with an <u>intensity</u> she had never been able to achieve in her own writing.

She glanced around. No one was watching. Without hesitation, she popped the disk out of the computer and put it in her purse. Dillon came in just as Jennifer was leaving.

"Hey!" she heard him say as she walked out the door. "What happened to the disk I was working on?"

Jennifer ignored him and hurried off.

"Jennifer, wait!" Dillon called after her. "I need to ask you something!"

Jennifer pretended not to hear him. "See you tomorrow, Dillon!" she called. Outside, she unlocked her bike and peeled out of the school lot. *What am I doing?* Jennifer thought, as she sped along the tree-lined streets toward her home. *I must be crazy to think I can get away with something like this. Dillon is bound to have other copies of his work.*

Then, suddenly, she heard the grinding of metal as someone rode up beside her. It was Dillon. How had he caught up to her on his crummy old one-speed bike?

"Wait up," he said breathlessly, his face red from pedaling hard. "I want to talk to you."

Jennifer ignored him. Eyes straight ahead, she downshifted a gear on her sleek, twenty-one-speed bike and shot ahead. But Dillon wasn't giving up. Within seconds he pulled up alongside her once more. "This won't do you any good!" he shouted.

Jennifer turned to look at him. They locked angry stares. Then Dillon looked back at the road ahead just in time to see a toddler chase a ball into the street.

intensity: a great deal of feeling

"Look out!" he shouted. Jennifer looked and froze. Dillon reached over and grabbed her handlebar to steer her away from the child. As he did, he lost control of his own bike, hit the curb, flipped, and came down hard. He was thrown twenty yards, and his unfastened helmet was torn away on impact.

Jennifer's bike hit a tree down the street across from the toddler, who watched the twin crashes with mild interest from midstreet, the ball safely in his hands.

Someone cried out and ran to call the paramedics. A crowd began to gather. Dazedly, Jennifer tried to pull herself away from her mangled bike. "Stay where you are," someone told her.

"Dillon?" She looked around.

His body lay stretched out on the grass nearby. His eyes were open, focused on her. His voice was faint but distinct. "What goes around comes around," he said, and then he smiled with a funny little twist of his lips.

Jennifer didn't know if he died then or on the way to the hospital. She was all right herself. A few bruises and a sore elbow were all she had to show for the accident.

"I saw the whole thing," said a heavyset man, getting out of his car. "The boy was chasing her," he told the gathering crowd, pointing to Jennifer. "He was yelling at her to wait, then he grabbed her handlebar and tried to make her stop."

Jennifer was sent to the hospital and held overnight for observation. She told the police who came to take her statement that she couldn't remember exactly what happened. "No," she said in answer to their questioning. "I don't know why he was chasing me."

The school delayed the writing competition deadline five days, until after Dillon's funeral. That was enough time for Jennifer to make Dillon's story over into her own. She attended the funeral with a long face, but a few hours later was sitting in front of her computer, copying Dillon's disk onto her <u>hard drive</u>. Then she hid the disk in a shoe box at the back of her closet.

Just as she knew it would, the story won the school competition, then went on to win at the state level. Although Jennifer's English teacher was surprised at the sudden forcefulness of her style, no one questioned the straight-A student.

Almost no one.

It was during Christmas vacation that Jennifer began to see Dillon out of the corner of her eye. In the mall or at the skating rink, there he was, watching her from a distance. He always wore a twisted smile, and he was always gone when she turned to look him full in the face.

The first phone call came in January, after Jennifer's story won the national competition and was printed in the local paper. "What goes around comes around," came the whispered words. It was Dillon's voice. Then there was only a dial tone. Jennifer took the phone off the hook, then closed all the drapes until her parents came home from work.

The next week at school, Jennifer saw Dillon standing in the doorway at the end of the hall. She recognized his

hard drive: the built-in memory of a computer, used for reading and writing information

Is it really Dillon? How could it be?

slouching walk, his leather jacket, and that horrible gash he'd gotten on his forehead from the accident.

"Look!" she said, clutching her friend Merilee's arm and pointing. But as suddenly as he had appeared, Dillon was gone.

"Look at what?" Merilee asked, running after Jennifer, who had reached the end of the hall and was looking wildly around the empty schoolyard.

"Didn't you see him?" Jennifer asked Merilee, her voice shaking.

"See who? There's nobody here. What's the matter with you lately?"

"You wouldn't understand," Jennifer snapped.

"Well, pardon me, your highness." Merilee moved off, muttering, "Winning contests sure changes some people."

From that time on, Jennifer began to watch for Dillon in earnest. She saw him once in the supermarket and once in the movie theater, but he always disappeared before she could get too close.

On Valentine's Day everyone in the class got a special valentine . . . everyone except Jennifer.

She heard about it from Merilee. "This was in my locker. Everybody's asking me what it means." She gave Jennifer a piece of paper the color of blood.

It was written like a poem. Jennifer read:

Our Jennifer would like to hide
the secret we have found,
but she's afraid because she knows
the truth will come around.

Beneath the poem was printed in crude block letters: "WHAT GOES AROUND COMES AROUND."

Jennifer stopped in her tracks in the center of the busy hall. Students pushed around her, rushing to class. She could see red sheets in their hands. Several turned to look at her. The blood drained from her face, and her knees felt ready to give way. Jennifer looked around. A group of girls was watching her.

Merilee took her aside. "Look, Jen. This is getting too weird. You have to tell me what's going on."

With an effort, Jennifer pulled herself together. "Nothing's going on. It's just somebody's idea of a joke." She turned and walked away, leaving Merilee staring after her, frowning.

Jennifer went straight to the nurse's office and asked to go home, pleading illness. She was, in fact, sick with fear, and her <u>ashen</u> face convinced the nurse. *How could they know?* she kept thinking, over and over again.

At home, she tore up the stairs and into her closet, throwing boxes aside until she found the one with Dillon's disk. She checked to make sure the disk was still there, then she put the box at the back of her closet behind everything that would fit in front of it.

Her mother came home from work to find Jennifer in bed with the lights out. "What's wrong, Jenny?" she asked. "Are you sick?"

"No, Mom. I just need some time alone." It had been their custom ever since Jennifer had been a little girl to talk over any problems she had, but this was one problem Jennifer couldn't tell anyone.

ashen: pale gray, like ashes

PREDICT

Do you think anyone will figure out Jennifer's secret?

Jennifer turned her back and pulled the pillow over her head.

The next day, Jennifer actually had a slight fever, so her mother let her stay home. Then it was the weekend, and she stayed in bed almost the whole time. On Monday, though, her mother insisted she go back to school. Luckily, by then the valentine letters had disappeared. Jennifer was able to pass them off as a practical joke, but her anxiety remained. She dreaded what would come next.

"The editor of the school yearbook wants you to write a story," her English teacher told her on Friday. "Along the lines of the one you wrote for the competition. It's a great honor to be asked to write for the annual, particularly since you're not a senior."

"Me?" Jennifer asked. The word came out like a strangled croak.

"I told them you would," the teacher said, smiling.

"You shouldn't have done that!" Jennifer blurted. Then, seeing the puzzled look the teacher gave her, she added, "I mean, I haven't been writing lately."

"I know. All the more reason for you to get back in gear. Consider it an English assignment."

"But . . ."

"I don't want to argue about this, Jennifer. I'll expect something by Monday."

At home later, Jennifer sat down at her computer and tried to write, but the words wouldn't come. She knew she couldn't write something like the winning entry. She might never be able to write anything again.

As she sat there, staring at the blank screen, her mother called to say she would be late and to please start dinner. "Your dad has to work late, so it'll be just the two of us," her mother said. "And, by the way, there's a surprise for you in the garage."

Jennifer shook her head and sighed as she stood in front of the brand-new bike in the garage. She picked up the card lying on the seat and read: *Cheer up, sweetheart. We love you, Mom & Dad.*

Nearly bursting into tears, Jennifer dropped the card and ran upstairs. She *had* to write something. She sat down at the computer, but once again nothing came to her. Then she had an idea.

She went to her closet, pulled out the shoe box, and retrieved Dillon's disk. She put it into the <u>A drive</u> and pulled the <u>directory</u> up on the screen. The first listing was the story she had stolen, and under that were several other documents that bore abbreviated titles she couldn't identify. Jennifer pulled one up. It was a list of colleges. She exited and tried again.

The second was somebody's homework, a history paper. She kept going. On the fifth try, she found something that looked like another story. She began to read—at first with interest, then with increasing horror.

In the story, a spoiled girl wanted to get into a certain college at any cost. She went so far as to steal a story from a classmate and enter it in a writing contest. She won, but the classmate exposed her act of <u>plagiarism</u> to the whole

A drive: one of the drives in a computer that reads the information stored on disks

directory: a list of the files stored on a computer

plagiarism: the act of taking someone else's ideas and presenting them as your own

school. The girl was expelled in disgrace, and her contest prize was stripped away. The moral of the story was contained in the last line, when the hero said to her, "What goes around comes around."

"*No!*" Jennifer screamed, snatching the disk from the drive and hurling it across the room. She threw herself across the bed, sobbing wildly. As she lay there, the phone rang. Jennifer debated whether to answer it and decided not to. But the ringing went on and on, and she finally snatched up the receiver. "Hello?"

Why is Jennifer so upset by this story?

"What goes around comes around," the voice breathed into the receiver.

"Dillon!" Jennifer cried. "Why are you doing this?" She sobbed and held the receiver away, staring at it. Then she dropped it and jumped up from the bed to search for the disk. Retrieving it from where it had fallen behind the nightstand, she fled to the garage.

Nearly flying as she sped away on her new bike, she barely missed a neighbor who was crossing the street. "Hey! Watch where you're going," he called after her as she raced off.

She knew exactly where she was going, but she was concentrating so hard on the traffic around her that she almost missed the turnoff to the cemetery. She sped through the gated entrance to the graveyard, trying to remember where Dillon's grave was.

At last she found the gravesite. It was at the top of the hill, in a section of new grass. She dropped her bike and threw herself to her knees with a sob. "I'm sorry, Dillon," she wailed. "Please forgive me." She took the disk from her coat pocket and dropped it on the ground. "Look! I've brought your disk. I'm going to give it back." She began digging at the earth with her bare hands. She was so intent on her task that she didn't hear the footsteps approaching from behind.

Suddenly, a black shadow loomed over her. She looked over her shoulder. There, his figure blocking the setting sun behind him, was Dillon.

Jennifer jumped to her feet with a scream. Dillon took a step toward her. She started to run.

"Wait," he said. "I want to talk to you."

Jennifer ran to her bike and raced down the hillside. She thought she heard someone riding behind her, but she dared not look back.

With a pounding heart, she pumped harder, flying out the cemetery gate and onto the street. *I know this part of town,* she thought frantically. *I can lose myself in one of the back streets.* Searching for a place to turn, she saw a movement out of the corner of her eye. Turning to look, she saw Dillon coming behind her, flashing the headlight on his bike. Jennifer pedaled with all her might, and her bike responded with a spurt of speed. She made it to the end of the block and turned right.

As she looked over her shoulder, she saw that Dillon was still behind her, and still gaining. She flew around the next corner. A station wagon was double-parked in the street, with children climbing out from all the doors. Jennifer hit the brakes and turned the front wheel sharply. The brakes locked, and her bike went out of control, plunging across the street into a telephone pole. Jennifer was thrown off and landed several feet away. She heard the

PREDICT

Will Jennifer escape from Dillon's ghost? What makes you think as you do?

sound of running steps, but she felt no pain. She fought for consciousness.

She looked up into Dillon's face. He took her hand. She could feel the warmth flow from his body into hers. She tried to focus, to speak.

"Don't try to talk."

The voice was like Dillon's, and yet it was not. His image was growing fuzzy. "You're not Dillon," she said. "Who are you?"

"His cousin."

Things were growing dark now, closing in around her, but she had to know. "How did you . . . ?"

"How did I know? I wouldn't have if the story hadn't won the contest and been published in the paper. You see, I wrote that story, not Dillon. I tried to talk to you back there at the cemetery, but you ran away."

She gave a little sigh. "What goes around . . ."

Her eyes closed, and Dillon's cousin moved out of the way of the paramedic who was vainly trying to find a pulse in Jennifer's lifeless body.

What Goes Around Comes Around

▼ Learning from the Story

Work with a group of three or four other students. Brainstorm ideas for another story based on the expression "What goes around comes around." Have one group member record your answers to the following questions.

- Who will be the main characters?
- Where will the story take place?
- What are three key events?

Share your group's ideas with other groups. How many different story ideas did your class get?

▼ Putting It into Practice

"What Goes Around Comes Around" is a story about a wish come true in a deadly way. Now it's your turn to dream up a story of a wish gone wrong. Make a list of three wishes that you'd like to make. Then list some events that might turn one of your wishes into a terrifying tale—a tale of a wish that *unfortunately* came true. You might explore more than one of your wishes to help you decide which one to turn into a story.

Beat Bart

Keep telling yourself, "It's only a game. It's only a game."

O liver dropped his book bag on the floor and plopped down onto his desk chair. He switched on his computer, punched the power button for the <u>monitor</u>, and waited while the hard drive checked itself for errors. After a moment, the computer beeped the "all-clear" and the monitor displayed a <u>simulated</u> desktop.

He slid the <u>mouse</u> until it was centered over the tiny telephone symbol and clicked the button. In seconds, he was in his communication software. He scrolled through the numbers in his phone book and selected the number for GameTime, a bulletin board he had recently discovered that catered especially to computer gamers.

When he was prompted, he entered his identification number and password. Then the standard greeting was displayed on the screen and the server waited for his response.

"Okay," Oliver said out loud, a habit he had developed while he was using the networks. "What's it going to be today?"

He decided to look in the section titled New Stuff. Posted there was an announcement for a brand-new

monitor: the part of a computer that includes the screen

simulated: made to look real

mouse: a small, moveable tool that controls the position of the cursor and the selection of functions on a computer interactive game which loudly claimed that it was BETTER THAN <u>VIRTUAL REALITY</u>!

"I doubt that," Oliver scoffed. But he called up the announcement on his screen anyway to see what it had to say for itself.

"BEAT BART," the announcement read. "The new generation of computer gaming. You've all experienced the hokey graphics and jerky movements of most other computer games. BEAT BART is as far removed from these clunkers as your computer is from a calculator. BEAT BART combines the newest advances in virtual reality programming with the high degree of personal involvement you get from interactive games. When you play BEAT BART, you're not just playing a computer simulation, you're playing against another person! Both of you in a computer-simulated setting that's so real you'll have trouble remembering it's 'only a game.'

"BEAT BART will be brought <u>on-line</u> in more than 100 different cities over the next month. BEAT BART is compatible with most <u>joysticks</u>, or you can order the BARTGUN from our on-line order number. If you try only one new game this year, make it BEAT BART. You'll never want to play another."

Oliver read through the list of dates that followed. "Excellent!" he yelled. His was one of the cities that would be part of the BEAT BART start-up. Marking the date on his desk calendar, Oliver moved on to the order line to buy the BARTGUN.

As the demonstration date drew closer, Oliver became nearly sleepless with excitement. His best friend, Rob, had

virtual reality: an artificial environment experienced through sights and sounds provided by a computer

on-line: connected to a computer system

joysticks: handlelike tools used to move the cursor around quickly on a computer screen

moved to the East Coast the summer before. Now Rob
lived in one of the cities where BEAT BART had made its
first appearance. The day after Rob tried it, he called Oliver.

"It's fantastic!" Rob promised. "You're not going to
believe it."

"How does it work?" Oliver demanded.

"It's really cool. But you gotta order the gun."

"I did." He didn't tell his friend that his parents had
almost refused to let him buy it, even though he had the
money saved up from his allowance. His dad thought there
were enough kids getting killed by real guns without
having games that centered around gunplay. It had been a
tough fight, but after Oliver had promised to mow the
lawn without ever complaining again, his dad gave in.

"The gun is what makes it happen," Rob went on
enthusiastically. "You gotta use it to shoot and to *see*."

"What do you mean, see?"

"Well, it's a bit weird at first, but you point the gun in
whatever direction you want to look and what you're
seeing shows up on your screen."

"Kind of like a mouse."

"Yeah. But a hundred times faster. No joke, you just
flick your wrist and the screen changes—it's that fast.
Takes a little getting used to."

"Is that how you move, too?"

"Nope. For that, you need your mouse. That was kind
of tough, too—using it with my left hand."

"Then what happens?"

"You pick whatever setting you want—I think there's
Old West, Big City, Futuristic, and a couple of others. I

*What makes this
computer game
"fantastic"?
How is it different
from other games?*

picked Old West, and it starts you off on the outskirts of a town. The whole point is to find and shoot the other guy before he shoots you. But the best part is that the other guys are other players."

"What?"

"Yeah! Somewhere there's someone else <u>logged on</u> and they're looking for you. That's what makes it so cool. You can play a hundred times and have a hundred different enemies."

"Is it tough?" Oliver asked.

"Not really," Rob said. "The guy I was going against didn't have a clue. I nailed him in the first five minutes. Then I played a couple more with some guys who were better, but I still won. I'm working my way up to Bart."

"Who's that?"

"Bart is the computer or, probably, the programmer. Anyway, after you have a certain number of kills, you go up against Bart."

After talking to Rob, Oliver could hardly wait for his own chance to beat Bart. Finally, the day arrived, and Oliver raced straight home from school. He wanted to get logged on fast in case there were a limited number of open ports. He waited impatiently for his computer to <u>boot</u>, then dialed the BEAT BART phone number.

"Welcome to BEAT BART," the screen flashed in bright red colors. "If you have bought a BARTGUN, please enter the serial number now."

Oliver did so and stared at the screen.

"Hello, Oliver. Are you ready to try your luck?"

"YES," Oliver typed.

logged on: connected to a computer network

boot: to start up

"Good. Please connect your BARTGUN if you have not already done so. Then <u>download</u> the file BART.EXE to your computer. It will require 275k of memory. When you are done, point the gun at the center of your screen and follow the on-screen instructions."

Oliver did as instructed, and once the program was in, he pointed the gun at the screen. Then he followed a set of exercises designed both to initiate his computer and to give him some practice on how to use the gun. Rob was right—it did take getting used to. Oliver had to keep reminding himself that "forward" was the direction his gun was pointing, so that he actually turned with the gun and not the mouse.

When he was finished practicing, the computer asked him to choose his setting. Smiling, he took aim at "Old West" and pulled the trigger.

"Please enter the name you would like to be known as, or type [Enter] for your own name."

Oliver thought a moment, then typed "MAD DOG."

"Okay, MAD DOG. Do you have a specific challenge in mind? Or are you open to all comers?"

The only other person Oliver knew was Rob, and he didn't know Rob's game name. He typed "OPEN."

His screen displayed a weathered signboard with the message, "You've just been informed that LEE THE KID has been seen riding for town. Last time you saw him he said you'd better be gone when he next came through town or he'd come hunting for you. The townspeople won't get involved, but they wish you luck." The signboard disappeared, and his screen showed an elevated view of an old western town.

download: to transfer information from one computer to another

Oliver stared at the monitor in surprise. The picture was so clear and crisp it seemed as if he was staring out a window. The only odd part was the <u>crosshairs</u> of the gunsight floating in midair. The hand holding his gun dropped to the desk.

Suddenly, the view tilted crazily and settled on a view of two feet in cowboy boots standing on dry, brown soil. With a disbelieving smile, Oliver slowly raised his hand and pointed the gun straight ahead. The view righted itself.

"All right," Oliver drawled in an excited whisper.

One hand resting gently on his mouse and the BARTGUN in his other, Mad Dog walked into town to face Lee the Kid.

By the time his mother called him for dinner, Oliver was a seasoned veteran of three gunfights. Contrary to what Rob had told him, he had come up against a pretty good player on his first outing. It was only through sheer luck that he had managed to win.

He had been walking through town, amazed at the way the screen changed perspective with such fluid ease. With a little imagination he really could believe he was walking down the dusty street of a western town. No matter where he pointed his gun there was something on the screen, even when he looked behind him. And there were people, too! The town was fully populated with men, women, and children who watched him solemnly as he gawked his way down Main Street. Some of them called out a greeting, which he heard through his computer speaker. "I'll have to get a sound board," Oliver noted to himself.

PREDICT

Do you think Oliver will beat Lee the Kid? What makes you think as you do?

crosshairs: thin lines that form a cross shape, used to line up a target

His sightseeing saved him in his first shoot-out. He had just passed a general store when he suddenly decided to see if the computer would allow him to enter it. He slid the mouse to take a quick step backwards. At that moment he heard the crack of a gunshot, and a chip of wood blasted away from the post next to his head.

Oliver jumped, and the monitor showed buildings, sky, and earth swirling madly as his hand waved the gun around. Meanwhile, his reaction slid the mouse all the way to one side, sending him flying backwards through the doorway of the store.

There was another shot, and the glass pane in the door shattered. Oliver managed to get his gun pointed out the window so he could look around.

Across the street was a man in dirty brown clothes. He was standing behind a post, sighting down his gun barrel at the door of the store. Without pausing to see if the man was in his sights, Oliver squeezed the trigger. There was a bang, and to his shock, he saw the man stagger out from behind the post.

Oliver had hit him in the shoulder, and blood was soaking the man's shirt. The man staggered forward, bringing up his gun to point it at Oliver. This time Oliver centered the crosshairs on the man's chest when he pulled the trigger. With a spray of blood, the man flew backwards to lie motionless in the street.

Suddenly, Oliver was back outside of town, facing the weathered signboard.

"Congratulations, MAD DOG. By ridding us all of scum like LEE THE KID, you have made Bartville a safer

place to live. You have one notch in your gun grip. Care to try for another?"

The next battle had lasted much longer, as both Oliver and his opponent spent most of their time sneaking around town, taking shots at each other rather than forcing an outright duel. Finally, Oliver shot the other player from a second-floor window.

The third battle was much the same, but this time Oliver tried running as fast as he could to the other side of town to get the drop on his man. It seemed to work—the enemy wasn't even paying attention when he walked by Oliver's hiding place.

Over the next few weeks, Oliver played BEAT BART as often as he could. He told all his friends at school about the game, but only one of them, Randy, had the required <u>hardware</u>. Oliver's parents were a little worried about his "<u>obsession</u>" with the game, but he was on his best behavior otherwise, so they let him continue.

Oliver called Rob sometimes to compare notes, but they made a promise never to tell each other their western names. "You'll know me when you fight me, though," said Rob. "I have a neat little trick that wins me about half the battles I'm in." He refused to tell Oliver any more than that.

They began an informal contest to see who could earn the most notches on his gun grip. As they each survived more and more battles, they raced neck and neck to the ultimate goal—to play against and beat Bart himself.

One day Randy swaggered theatrically up to Oliver on the playground. "You varmint," he said in his best imitation of a Wild West gunslinger, "I'm calling you out!"

hardware: the equipment—monitor, keyboard, mouse, etc.—of a computer

obsession: something taking up all one's thoughts and time

Oliver answered with a fierce scowl. "Name the time, you fleabitten dog."

"Tonight. Eight o'clock. If you ain't yellow."

"I'll be there," Oliver nodded. "What's your name, stranger? So's I can get it right on your tombstone."

"Folks call me 'Killer.'"

"Well, Killer, you've just run up against Mad Dog. And tonight at eight, you're gonna get bit!"

That was too much for Randy, and he burst out laughing. Oliver dropped his mean look and joined in.

"So how do we do this?" Randy asked.

"I'm not sure. I guess when you log on, you specify that you want a challenge. When it asks for a name, type Mad Dog."

"Got it, Mad Dog. I'll be waiting on-line at eight o'clock."

"See you in Bartville," Oliver agreed.

It wasn't until Oliver logged on that night that he realized how close he was to having enough notches to challenge Bart. By pure chance, winning this battle against Randy would put him in the eligible column. "If you do," he reminded himself grimly.

The signboard informed him that a challenge had been issued by KILLER and asked if he wanted to accept it. Excited and nervous, Oliver entered "YES."

It seemed like ages before he logged off. Randy had been good—real good. For a time Oliver had really been worried that he wouldn't be able to beat his friend. Bad enough that he would have had to start over on the path to Bart. But to have to face Randy the next day would have been unbearable.

PREDICT

Was your last prediction right? Who do you think will win this round— Mad Dog Oliver or Killer Randy? Why?

Oliver sat back and felt his sweat-drenched shirt against his skin. The long battle had ended pretty spectacularly. He had aimed and fired in one motion, and had managed to hit Killer smack in the gun hand. With a vivid spray of blood, Killer's right hand had been ruined. When Randy tried to run, Oliver chased after him and plugged him in the back as he was sprinting down the street.

Of course Oliver would never ever admit to Randy that his first shot had been pure luck—he had really been aiming for Killer's chest!

The next day at school he waited out front for the ex-Killer, but Randy didn't show up. He wasn't at lunch, either, and Oliver began to suspect he was so embarrassed he had skipped school.

"He's not going to get away with that," Oliver promised himself. After school he rode over to Randy's house. He rang the doorbell and stood on the porch, flashing a big, triumphant grin.

Randy's father opened the door. He looked awful, pale with dark circles under his eyes. His clothes were all wrinkled, as if he had slept in them, but he didn't look as if he had slept at all.

"Uh, hi, Mister Reese," Oliver said. "Is Randy home?"

Mr. Reese looked at Oliver for a long moment, as if he were trying to place the familiar face. Then he said slowly, "Oliver. Randy was killed last night."

Oliver's eyes bugged out. He felt like his jaw was about to hit his knees. "What? How? I mean . . . I'm sorry but, well . . . Mister Reese, how did it happen?"

Randy's father answered in a voice as dead as his son. "We don't know. We found him this morning in his bedroom, shot."

A small, cold hand seemed to run its fingers along Oliver's spine. "Shot?" he squeaked.

"That's right," Mr. Reese said in his dull voice. "Right in his own room. We didn't hear a thing, but we found him there this morning."

Oliver gulped and shook his head a little to clear his ears. Even as he asked the next question, he told himself that what he was thinking just wasn't possible.

"Where—where was he shot?" he asked in a small voice.

Mr. Reese's mouth stretched in a ghastly imitation of a smile. "That's the strange part, you know? He was shot twice. Once in the hand and once, according to the police doctor, in the back."

Oliver mumbled something and stumbled away from the door. He groped blindly for his bike and turned for home.

"It's just not possible!" he told himself. "It must be some sort of crazy <u>coincidence</u>!" But what kind of coincidence could explain a thirteen-year-old kid being shot for no reason, in the middle of his room, in exactly the same places Oliver had shot him in a computer game the night before?

He stopped pedaling and coasted to a stop in front of his house. If what he was thinking was true, then what about all those other people he had killed while playing BEAT BART? Even worse, what about all the other people who were playing? Shivers racked his body as his

coincidence: an event that happens at the same time as another by accident

mind began to add up the numbers. Randy's death had to be a coincidence. It had to be.

Oliver made his way to the phone and called Rob. There was no answer, even though it was later in the evening on Rob's end. He hung up and went to his room.

He found himself staring at the BEAT BART signboard. He had no memory of sitting down and logging on, but the suddenly eerie signboard was there on his screen.

"Congratulations, MAD DOG," the signboard read. "You are now eligible to challenge Bart for the title of Master Gunslinger. Do you wish to challenge Bart now?"

Oliver stared at the screen so long his <u>screen saver</u> winked on. If it was just a game, then he was acting like an idiot. But if, somehow, it was not, he might be risking his life. Thoughts swirling, he deliberately aimed and shot out the word "YES." He had to try to kill Bart—to save all the others who were playing this horrible game.

Like all the others, the game began with Oliver on the outskirts of town. More cautious than ever, he carefully made his way into Bartville.

Long before, Oliver had discovered that a player didn't have to approach town in a direct line from where the game began. His usual practice was to circle around to the opposite side of town. Sometimes, when he was lucky, he could come up behind the other player and the battle would be over before it had even begun.

This time, however, something occurred that had never happened before. As he was making his way in a large <u>circuit</u> around Bartville, he saw another man doing the

Did you predict that this would happen? How does this development change your opinion of the game?

What would you do if you were Oliver? Why?

screen saver: a moving image that appears on a computer screen if the computer is not used for a few minutes

circuit: a trip around

same! Moving quickly, Oliver jumped down into a gully and raced in the opposite direction.

Bart is good! he thought frantically. And if he was too good, what did that mean for Oliver?

Time passed without meaning as Oliver and Bart moved in an intricate dance through and around Bartville. Every now and then one would catch a glimpse of the other, and shots would crack over the speaker. But neither fighter was able to get a bead on his opponent.

Then, on as simple a thing as turning a corner a second before the other gunman, the match was over. Oliver's bullet took Bart just to the right of the middle of his chest. The other gunman seemed to get drawn up onto his toes, where he balanced for an instant before slowly toppling over like a cut tree.

Wearily, Oliver let his gun drop down, and the screen obligingly showed him the dirt at his feet. After a moment, he realized how odd that was. At the end of every other battle he had been instantly presented with the signboard on the outskirts of town. This time, he remained standing in the street.

Raising his gun, he looked around. A crowd was cautiously gathering in a rough oval around him and the fallen Bart. Suddenly curious to see what face the computer gave itself, Oliver walked over to the dead body.

His breath caught in his throat and he gasped. "No!" Lying in a patch of bloody mud was Rob. His eyes stared upwards, and he blinked when Oliver came into his field of vision.

"Congratulations, Bart," he whispered. Then his eyes slowly rolled back in his head.

"That's right, son," said the old man who was standing next to Oliver. He clapped a friendly hand on Oliver's arm and *Oliver felt it*. "Now you're the Master Gunslinger. Glad to have you with us."

Oliver could smell the dusty air and feel the warm sun on his back. He could hear the townspeople murmuring. The old man looked down at Rob's lifeless body, then back up at Oliver. "Sure hope you last longer than that one did."

Who did Bart turn out to be? What are the rules of the game?

Beat Bart

▼ Learning from the Story

It's obvious that the author of "Beat Bart" knows something about computers. Working with a partner, make a list of all the terms in this story related to computers. As you find the terms, define them for each other. Share your list with the class and discuss the terms and their meanings.

▼ Putting It into Practice

To explore ideas for your story, think about how you're going to get from the beginning to the end. As you plan each part, try freewriting, sketching, listing, or using charts or webs to get your ideas on paper. Write down any ideas. Use your imagination freely.

Beginning—Describe the characters and setting. Think about what problem the characters will face.
Middle—List the events of the plot in the order they will happen.
Ending—How will the story end? Will the characters solve the problem, or will the ending be a surprise to everyone, maybe even to you?

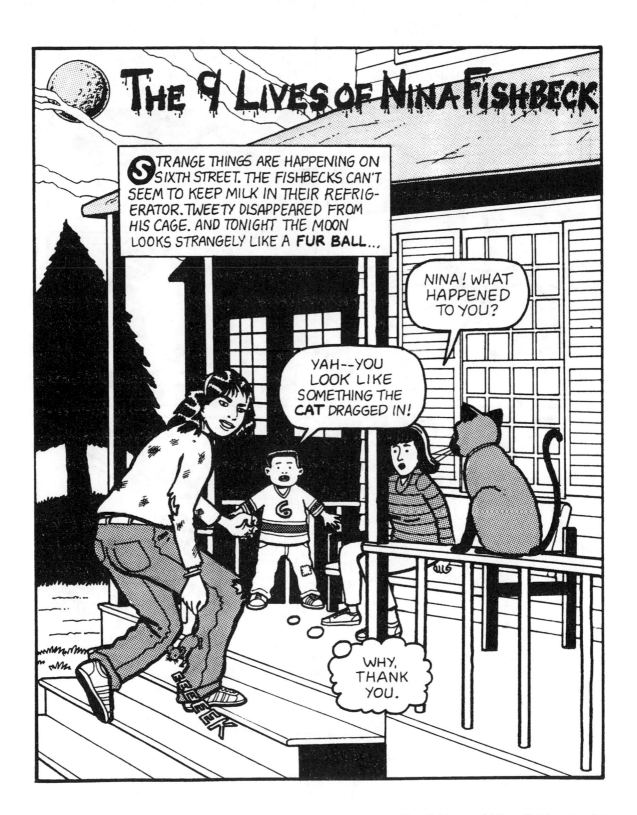

The 9 Lives of Nina Fishbeck

▼ Learning from the Story

A good comic book doesn't just *tell* you what's happening, it *shows* you. To understand the difference between showing and telling, try the following experiment. Tell a partner how to do something— maybe how to play a new video game, how to draw a cartoon character, or how to tie his or her shoes. Don't use any visuals or hand gestures; just explain the steps involved. Then *show* your partner how to do the task. Demonstrate the steps, using props or drawings. Ask which way was more helpful and why.

▼ Putting It into Practice

Plan to put your "wish" story into a comic book format. To do this, you need to start with a script. A comic book script includes ideas for the cartoon drawings as well as ideas for the words the characters will say.

Make a list of the events you've decided on for your story. For each event, write directions for drawing a panel to show the action. Remember that it is more interesting to show people actively doing something than it is to show them talking. If you can't draw, don't worry. You can work with a partner. What's important is giving a clear description of what the drawing should include to move your story along.

THE SUBSTITUTION

Have you ever **wished** that one of your teachers would just **disappear?** Substitutes couldn't possibly be any worse— **or could they?**

Mr. Grunchmacher cleared his throat. "I don't mean to disturb you, Kate," he said sarcastically, "but could you tell the class about the Turner Thesis?"

Thirteen-year-old Kate Krabbe looked up from the doodles she'd been making in her notebook. From a series of disconnected squares and triangles, she had artistically fashioned a huge, dinosaurlike monster straight out of an old Japanese horror movie. If a psychiatrist were to see this and the other horrific drawings in Kate's notebook, he might conclude that the girl had a very sick and twisted imagination. But to Kate the drawings merely represented the normal frustrations of a healthy, all-American girl who was bored silly with American history. At least, she was bored with the way Mr. Grunchmacher taught it.

"The Turner Thesis, Kate?" her stern, gray-haired teacher repeated impatiently.

"Um, could you rephrase the question?" Kate asked innocently.

"Do you know what the Turner Thesis is?" Mr. Grunchmacher said through clenched teeth. "Manifest

Destiny? Westward expansion? Does any of this sound familiar, or have I been wasting my time?"

Kate sank into her chair and <u>averted</u> her eyes. The truth was, she had no idea what Mr. Grunchmacher was talking about but felt it was better to stay silent rather than admit she'd been daydreaming for the entire period.

Mr. Grunchmacher heaved a frustrated sigh, then turned to address the other students, who looked just as lost as Kate. "You know, education is a two-way street. I can stand up here and talk all I want, but it's not going to do a bit of good unless you choose to pay attention. You have to *want* to learn. You have to make an *effort*. I can't do it all myself."

"Oh, yeah?" Kate cried, suddenly leaping to her feet. "Well, maybe we would pay attention if you said something *interesting*! If you didn't babble on and on about things that didn't make any difference today!"

Actually, Kate didn't really say this. She *wanted* to say it. She was *desperate* to say it. But a combination of fear, shyness, and, perhaps, common sense prevented her from doing so. Instead, she just sank lower and lower into her chair and silently wished that Mr. Grunchmacher would simply vanish off the face of the earth. Maybe then school might not be the living nightmare she currently found it to be.

"All right, Kate," Mr. Grunchmacher said, returning his attention to her alone. "Just to show me that my efforts have not been totally wasted, I want a five-page report from you on the Turner Thesis on my desk tomorrow morning."

"But I can't—" Kate began.

"There's no such word as *can't* in my classroom," Mr. Grunchmacher snapped, cutting her off. "You have to

averted: turned away

demand one hundred percent from yourself. Remember, success only comes from high expectations."

"Yes, sir," Kate grumbled, secretly wishing for the day when the old geezer would finally be out of her life forever.

"Mr. Grunchmacher has got to be at least sixty years old," Kate's friend Zoe LaGrange noted as the two of them rode the bus home from school that afternoon. "<u>Statistically</u> speaking, he could drop dead at any time."

Zoe was also in Mr. Grunchmacher's class and shared Kate's extreme dislike of the man.

"I don't want him to die," Kate insisted. "I just want him to go away. You know, like retire. Move to Bora Bora or something."

"It's not gonna happen," Zoe stated. "We're not that lucky."

Kate figured that if Mr. Grunchmacher wasn't going to disappear, then at least *she* could come down with the flu and not have to go to school for the rest of the week. Yes, even headaches, muscle aches, chills, and nausea were starting to look better than a single day with that awful old teacher.

Unfortunately, the next morning Kate was in perfect health. She had no choice but to get dressed, have breakfast, pack up her books, and catch the bus to school. Sitting with Zoe, Kate was halfway to Wendell Wilkie Junior High when she realized, much to her horror, that she'd completely forgotten about the paper Mr. Grunchmacher had assigned her to write.

PREDICT

What do you think might happen as a result of Kate's secret wish?

statistically: based mathematically on numbers and averages

"Mr. Grunchmacher is going to eat you alive!" Zoe exclaimed after Kate told her about the mistake. "Boy, I'd hate to be in your shoes."

"Maybe he forgot about it," Kate said hopefully.

"Not likely," Zoe said with a <u>ghoulish</u> laugh. "He's still after my big brother Jack about a social studies paper he forgot to turn in—and that was five years ago!"

Kate's legs were trembling with fear when she entered her homeroom class and took her usual seat. As class time approached, she sank even lower than normal in her chair, hoping that when he arrived, Mr. Grunchmacher wouldn't notice her.

And then, at 8:30 A.M. on the nose, something unexpected happened. Mr. Grunchmacher failed to appear. Five minutes later, the teacher was still nowhere to be seen.

He's not coming! thought Kate, joy rising in her heart. *Maybe he had car trouble, or he's sick, or maybe—he actually disappeared!*

Kate was still imagining all the possible reasons for Mr. Grunchmacher's absence when a young, handsome man with thick black hair strode into the classroom and stopped in front of the teacher's desk.

"May I have your attention, please," he said with a dazzling smile, his voice as wonderful as he was. "My name is Mr. Wintergreen. I'll be your substitute today."

For the first time in weeks, Kate actually bolted up straight in her chair, both stunned by the wonderful news and impressed by the substitute's good looks. Then she slowly raised her hand. "Uh, excuse me," she said. "But is Mr. Grunchmacher sick?"

ghoulish: horrible

"To tell you the truth, I really don't know," Mr. Wintergreen admitted. "Your principal, Mrs. Wilhite, called me about an hour ago and asked me to come in. Now, let's get to our work, shall we?"

Over the next forty minutes, a miracle happened. For the first time since she entered the seventh grade, Kate Krabbe paid attention during a history lecture. Even more amazing, she actually *enjoyed* it. Unlike Mr. Grunchmacher, who always spoke in the same dull, uninspired <u>monotone</u> and who always got bogged down in endless, unimportant details, Mr. Wintergreen taught the class with the energy and enthusiasm of a stage actor. Talking about historical ideas, attitudes, and emotions in such a way that it made Kate actually *feel* something for the period he was talking about, the substitute actually made her *eager* to learn more. And after school, she found out that Zoe felt the same way.

"Isn't Mr. Wintergreen the greatest?" Zoe exclaimed as the two rode home on the bus later that day after school. "I mean, I actually *care* about the American pioneers!"

"On a scale of one to ten, I'd say he's a solid twenty-five!" Kate replied. Then her expression darkened. "I hope this isn't his only day. I mean, if Mr. Grunchmacher comes back tomorrow, I don't think I'll be able to stand it."

"I know," Zoe agreed. "Just one day, and we've been spoiled!"

"For life," Kate added. Turning to the window, she silently wished that Mr. Grunchmacher would *never* come back, that Mr. Wintergreen would be her homeroom teacher for the rest of the semester. Of course she realized

What do you think happened to Mr. Grunchmacher?

monotone: speaking in the same one tone or sound

that was too much to expect. But then, as Mr. Grunchmacher was fond of saying, success only comes from high expectations.

The next morning Kate crept cautiously into her classroom like a young medieval princess entering the lair of a deadly dragon. Although she fervently hoped that Mr. Wintergreen would return, she knew it was far more likely that Mr. Grunchmacher would be back, his recent illness having made him meaner and more <u>ornery</u> than ever.

But, to her delight, she found Mr. Wintergreen seated at the desk, preparing his notes for the day.

"Hi, Mr. Wintergreen!" Kate said with a smile. "I'm really glad you're back."

"I'm happy to be here," he replied warmly. "Everyone here has been so nice to me. And the class is so attentive. It makes teaching a pleasure."

"Well, you make learning a pleasure," Kate said, blushing when she realized that she sounded like a teacher's pet. Embarrassed, she hurried to her desk.

When the bell rang three minutes later and all the students had taken their seats, Mr. Wintergreen closed the door and began his instruction.

"First of all, I'd like to announce that Wendy Radcliffe and Joseph Morgenstern are no longer in this class," he said pleasantly.

Kate perked up in surprise. Although she didn't know either Wendy or Joseph very well—both of the kids had been goof-offs who'd kept pretty much to themselves—she

ornery: irritating; difficult to deal with

hadn't heard any talk about either of them moving or transferring to another school.

"In their place, I'd like to welcome two new students to our class," the substitute teacher went on in his deep voice. "Let's say hello to Vicky Carswell and Bradley McShane."

Kate and the other kids turned to see two new kids sitting at Wendy's and Joseph's old desks. Both kids were unusually good-looking and perfectly dressed. Together, they nodded to the class and flashed identical, picture-perfect smiles.

"Now, let's get back to American history, shall we?" said Mr. Wintergreen, opening his textbook. "Today I'd like to discuss the conflicts between the European settlers and the Native Americans."

Again, Mr. Wintergreen launched into a wonderful history lecture. But this time, Kate's attention started to wander. She couldn't help but glance back at the new kids, wondering where they might have come from and where Wendy and Joseph had gone.

"Don't you think it's weird that these two new kids showed up on the same day Wendy and Joseph left?" Kate asked Zoe during their bus ride home.

"A little," Zoe agreed. "But weird things happen. Like those twins who were separated at birth, grew up in totally different parts of the country, and ended up living right next door to each other!"

"What's your point?" Kate demanded impatiently.

"I'm just saying, don't sweat it," Zoe advised. "This is a weird world. But that's no reason to get all <u>paranoid</u>."

Why do you think Wendy Radcliffe and Joseph Morgenstern are gone?

paranoid: overly suspicious

Kate decided to take her friend's advice—until the next morning when she found that five more students in her class had been "substituted" by new kids. All of them were good-looking, perfectly groomed, sweet-natured, and unfailingly cheery . . . just like the amazing Mr. Wintergreen.

This time even Zoe had to admit that something seriously weird was going on. Sitting at their cafeteria table during lunch, the two girls discussed what their next move should be.

"We have to talk to the principal," Zoe insisted. "She's bound to know what's going on."

"But what if the principal is in on it?" Kate asked. "*She's* the one who called Mr. Wintergreen in the first place. Maybe Mrs. Wilhite is just using Mr. Wintergreen to—"

"To *what*?" Zoe demanded, getting upset. "All we know is that new kids are replacing old ones."

"Just like Mr. Grunchmacher was replaced," Kate said. And then it hit her. "Zoe, think about this. So far, who has disappeared? First it was Mr. Grunchmacher, someone no one could stand. Then it was Wendy Radcliffe and Joseph Morgenstern, two of the worst students in the class."

"Even worse than we are," Zoe noted.

"That's right, even worse than we are," Kate agreed, her agitation rising. "Then five more kids went, and none of them were exactly straight-A students."

"So what are you saying, Kate?" Zoe asked, her eyes filled with fear. "That they're getting rid of all the bad students and replacing them with good ones? That maybe we'll be next?"

"Could be," said Kate, now glancing around as if half-expecting someone to be creeping up behind her with a <u>sledgehammer</u> and a butterfly net. "Maybe this is their way of raising the school's test averages. By getting rid of all the losers, maybe they can get more money from the school board or something."

"Okay, but what happens to all the bad students?" asked Zoe. "What do they do, send them to another school? Throw them into a big pit? What?"

"Unless we get our grades up really fast, something tells me we'll soon find out," Kate replied grimly.

The next morning Kate headed off to school feeling like a <u>condemned</u> woman about to face a firing squad. From the moment she stepped out her front door she kept her eyes fixed forward, her face frozen in an expression of dark <u>determination</u> as she struggled to mentally prepare herself for whatever awful fate lay ahead.

Aboard the school bus, she rode alone. Zoe LaGrange had not gotten on at her usual stop, indicating to Kate that whatever forces were making the students of Mr. Grunchmacher's class disappear had already gotten to her friend. Her feelings of dread rose again when she walked stiffly into her class and saw a tall, well-dressed girl sitting in Zoe's usual chair. In fact, the classroom was now filled with cute, squeaky-clean kids, all of whom had the same perfect posture, the same attentive expressions, and the same achingly sweet, pearly-white smiles. There wasn't a familiar face among them.

What did you learn from the girls' conversation?

sledgehammer: a large, heavy hammer

condemned: sentenced to die

determination: firmness

"Come on in, Kate," Mr. Wintergreen called from his desk. "We're all just dying to get started today."

With this, Kate snapped. Spinning on her heels, she bolted like a madwoman down the hall, <u>vaulted</u> down the stairs, and burst into the administration office.

"I've got to talk to Principal Wilhite!" she gasped to the three startled-looking secretaries. "It's a matter of life or death!"

"I'm sorry," one of the secretaries replied. "But Mrs. Wilhite isn't with us anymore."

The next moment the door to the principal's office opened and a stunningly beautiful woman wearing a perfectly tailored designer suit and a movie-star smile stepped into view.

"Why, hello, Kate," she said in a rich, musical voice. "I'm the new principal, Ms. Cornflower. And I've been waiting for you." She reached her perfectly manicured fingers toward Kate.

"Noooooooo!" Kate screamed. "I am not going to be substituted."

Turning around, she bolted back out into the hall, sprinted to the school's main entrance, threw open the front door, ran down the front steps . . . and suddenly found herself tumbling through a black <u>void</u>.

Kicking her arms and legs wildly as a cold wind whipped past her face, Kate turned and looked up in terror to see her school getting smaller and smaller, like a picture disappearing into a bottomless well. Only it was Kate who was falling and who would likely continue to fall until the end of time. For as the last bit of light vanished above her

vaulted: jumped; leapt

void: an empty space

and she found herself <u>enveloped</u> in frigid blackness, Kate realized that through a combination of forces she would likely never understand, she had in fact just disappeared off the edge of the earth.

"So who can tell me about the Turner Thesis?" Mr. Wintergreen asked his class of attentive seventh graders. Every hand in the room went up. He pointed to the student seated in the second row of the third aisle. "Tabitha?"

Tabitha Miller, the cute, well-dressed girl who sat at the desk once occupied by the now-forgotten Kate Krabbe, smiled brightly as she began to discuss nineteenth-century historian Frederick Turner and his ideas about the American frontier. The other students, all of whom were just as attractive and sharply attired as Tabitha, listened with <u>rapt</u> attention. They were all perfect students with a perfect teacher in what had finally become a perfect class.

Meanwhile, somewhere far, far away, Kate Krabbe sank lower and lower into her seat. There, at the front of a classroom identical to the one she'd been miserable in at Wendell Wilkie Junior High, was old Mr. Grunchmacher babbling on and on about things she'd never care about or understand, even if she lived for a million years. And in this new world—identical to the one Kate had just disappeared from, except for the perfect people that had replaced her and her doomed classmates—living for a million years was eminently possible.

PREDICT

Is Kate lost forever? Where did she go? What will it be like there?

enveloped: wrapped; surrounded

rapt: spellbound; engrossed

THE SUBSTITUTION

▼ Learning from the Story

"The Substitution" uses some dialogue to tell the story. But in comic books, usually the only words are dialogue. Working with a partner, turn any page from "The Substitution" into a comic book page. You might find that in some cases you need to add dialogue, while in other cases you may have to make a conversation shorter.

▼ Putting It into Practice

How are you going to tell your story? Remember, most of the story in a comic book is told through dialogue. Create some dialogue for your story. Remember that you will have only what the characters say and the pictures to tell your story. Make the dialogue sound like real speech. You can test your dialogue by recording it and listening to find out how it sounds. Better yet, act out the story with a friend or two while the tape recorder runs.

The Magical Marker

At first Tamara thought it was <u>coincidence</u>. She drew a picture of her family on a carousel, and that night, amazingly, her dad announced they were going to the amusement park. But she became suspicious when, two days after using the *same* marker to draw a picture of herself kissing Steve, the boy of her dreams, he asked *her* to go steady! And when she drew a picture of an elephant trumpeting its way down Main Street and the next day a real elephant escaped from the circus and marched through downtown, she knew there was no doubt—the marker she was using was magical.

"Wow!" she said, staring at the seemingly ordinary marker. "Okay, Mr. Magic, let's see what you can *really* do." And she set to work drawing her family living in a huge mansion.

She had barely finished drawing the swimming pool when her dad, who *never* played the lottery, walked in waving a winning ticket. Tamara was the only one who wasn't surprised. They moved into a mansion less than a week later.

During the next few months, Tamara drew pictures of herself getting straight A's, sailing on a pirate ship, and

Wouldn't it be great if everything you ever wished for came true? Get real!

coincidence: an event that happens at the same time as another by accident

being a secret agent. And everything she drew came true in one way or another—the A's came by way of a computer glitch; she was asked to play a pirate in the school play; and her older sister gave her five dollars to spy on her new boyfriend. *So why not shoot for the moon?* she thought, drawing herself as an astronaut. Sure enough, two days later, the president himself picked Tamara from a list of kids to ride in the space shuttle.

Tamara was very happy. She had everything she desired. And if she desired anything else, she knew she could just draw it.

But one day Tamara realized with a shock that the marker was running out of ink. She'd never considered that that might happen. Then she had a great idea. Clutching the marker, she drew a picture of the world. Then, just as the marker ran dry, she drew herself sitting on top of the world wearing a crown. Content that she'd drawn the ultimate wish, she confidently flipped on the television and waited for the announcement of her <u>coronation</u>.

But the screen had only a very dim picture. In fact, everything in the room was growing dim . . . and things seemed to be moving farther away. Something else was happening, too. She was having trouble breathing! The air was being sucked right out of her lungs as if a vacuum cleaner were attached to them. And she was cold, *very* cold.

Where am I? she thought frantically. And just as everything started to go black, she felt the earth under her feet and the crown on her head, and nothing else . . . nothing else at all.

PREDICT

Uh oh! Things are going too well for Tamara. What do you think might go wrong?

coronation: a ceremony in which a king or queen is crowned

▼ Learning from the Story

"The Magical Marker" is told from a third-person point of view—the narrator is someone outside the story. When the narrator is a character in a story, the story is being told from a first-person point of view. Working with a partner, make a list of the third-person pronouns used in "The Magical Marker." Then take turns reading parts of the story, substituting pronouns so it is told from a first-person point of view. As you read, have your partner list the pronouns you use.

▼ Putting It into Practice

Work with two classmates. Let one person be the "main character." Have each team member take notes on what happens to that person for 10 minutes during lunch.

- The main character writes about everything he or she does, thinks, or feels.
- One person observes the main character and writes about everything she or he does.
- Another person writes about *everything* that happens—to the main character and to everyone else he or she sees during the 10 minutes.

Compare the three versions of what happened. How does the point of view change the story?

Same Time Next Year

It's a law of physics that opposites attract. But what exactly do they attract?

In a vast universe, toward the edge of a spinning galaxy, on a small blue planet flying around the sun, in a place called Northern California, lives a girl who is quite certain that the entire universe revolves around her. Or at least she acts that way. In fact, if an award were given out for acting superior, Marla Nixbok would win it.

"I was born a hundred years too early," she often tells her friends. "I ought to be living in a future time where I wouldn't be surrounded by such dweebs."

To prove that she is ahead of her time, Marla always wears next year's fashions and hairstyles that seem just a bit too weird for today. In a college town known for being on the cutting edge of everything, Marla is quite simply the Queen of Fads at Palo Alto Junior High. Nothing and nobody is good enough for her, and for that reason alone, everyone wants to be her friend.

Except for the new kid, Buford, who couldn't care less.

Buford and Marla meet on the school bus. It's his first day. As fate would have it, the seat next to Marla is the only free seat on the bus.

The second he sits down, Marla's nose tilts up, and she begins her usual grading process of new kids.

"Your hair is way greasy," she says. "Your clothes look like something out of the fifties, and in general, you look like a <u>Neanderthal</u>."

Several girls behind them laugh.

"All else considered, I give you an F as a human being."

He just smiles, not caring about Marla's grade. "Hi, I'm Buford," he says, ignoring how the girls start laughing again. "But you can call me Ford. Ford Planct."

Ford, thinks Marla. She actually likes the name, against her best instincts. "Okay, F-plus—but just because you got rid of the 'Bu' and called yourself 'Ford.'"

"Didn't you move into the old Wilmington place?" asks a kid in front of them.

"Yeah," says Buford.

The kid snickers. "Sucker!"

"Why? What's wrong with the place?" asks Ford, innocently.

"Nothing," says Marla, "except for the fact that it used to belong to Dr. Wilmington, the creepiest professor Stanford University ever had."

Ford leans in closer to listen.

"One day," says Marla, "about seven years ago, Wilmington went into the house . . . and never came out." Then she whispers, "No one ever found his body."

Ford nods, not showing a bit of fear.

"Personally," says Marla, trying to get a rise out of him, "I think he was killed by an ax murderer or something, and he's buried in the basement."

Neanderthal: an early Stone Age human being

But Ford only smiles. "I wouldn't be surprised," he says. "There's a whole lot of weird things down in our basement."

Marla perks up. "Oh, yeah? What sort of things?"

"Experimental things, I guess. Gadgets and stuff. Does anyone know what sort of research this Professor Wilmington was doing when he disappeared?"

No one on the bus responds.

Ford smiles and then stares straight at Marla. "By the way," he says, pointing to her purple-tinted hair and neon eye shadow, "you've got to be the weirdest-looking human being I've ever seen."

Marla softens just a bit. "Why, thank you, Ford!"

What details does the author include that help you get a mental picture of Marla and Ford?

Marla peers out of her window that night. Through the dense oak trees she can see the old Wilmington house farther down the street. A light is on in an upstairs window. She wonders if it's Ford's room.

Like Marla, Ford is trapped out of his time, only *he* belongs in the past, and she belongs in the future. It's not as if she likes him or anything. How could she like him— he is a full geek-o-rama nausea-fest. But she can use him. She can use him to get a look at all those dark, mysterious machines in his basement.

Marla smiles at the thought. Using people is a way of life for her.

And so the very next afternoon, Marla fights a blustery wind to get to Ford's house. By the time she arrives, her punked-out hair looks worse than ever, for the wind has stood every strand on end. She likes it even better now.

"Thanks for coming over to help me study," says Ford as he lets her in. "I mean, moving in the middle of the school year sure makes it hard to catch up."

"Well, that's just the kind of person I am," says Marla. "Anything I can do to help a friend."

Marla looks around. The furniture is so tacky it makes her want to gag. The living room sofa is encased in a plastic slipcover. Ford's mother vacuums the carpet wearing a polka-dot dress, like in "I Love Lucy." For Marla, it's worse than being in a room filled with snakes.

"It's noisy here," says Ford. "Let's go study in my room."

Marla shudders. Who knows what terrors she'll find there?

"How about the basement?" she asks.

"It's creepy down there," says Ford.

"You're not scared, are you?"

"Who, me? Naw."

Marla gently takes his hand. "C'mon, Ford . . . we need a nice quiet place to study."

Ford, who has taken great pains not to be affected by the things Marla says or does, finally loses the battle. He takes one look at her hand holding his and begins to blush through his freckles. "Oh, all right."

While the rest of the house has been repainted and <u>renovated</u>, the basement has not changed since the day Wilmington disappeared. All of the old man's bizarre stuff is down there. Maybe Wilmington himself is down there somewhere, just a dried-out old skeleton lurking behind a heavy machine. What if they were to find him? How cool would that be?

What kind of person is Marla? Do you like her? Why or why not?

renovated: restored; made new again

As they descend the rickety stairs, Marla grips Ford's hand tightly, not even realizing she is doing so. Ford's blush deepens.

"Gosh, I thought you didn't even like me," says Ford.

Marla ignores him, blocking out the thought, and looks around. "What is all this stuff?"

"That's what I've been trying to figure out," says Ford.

Everything is <u>shrouded</u> in sheets and plastic tarps. Strange shapes bulge out. They look like ghosts, lit by the flickering fluorescent light. There is a warped wooden table in the middle of it all. Ford drops his schoolbooks on the table, and a cloud of dust rises. It smells like death down there—all damp and moldy. The walls are covered with peeling moss, and they ooze with moisture.

"We can study here," says Ford, patting the table. But Marla is already pulling the sheets off the machines.

Whoosh! A sheet flutters off with an explosion of dust, revealing a dark, metallic, multiarmed thing that looks like some ancient torture device.

"I wouldn't touch that," says Ford.

Marla crooks her finger, beckoning him closer. Her nails are painted neon pink and blue with tiny rhinestones in the center of each one. She leans over and whispers in Ford's ear, "If you really want to be my friend, you'll help me uncover all these machines."

Ford, his blush turning even deeper, begins to rip off the sheets.

When they're done, a cloud of dust hangs in the air like fog over a swamp, and the machines within that dusty

shrouded: covered

Why is Ford blushing? How is Marla getting him to do what she wants?

swamp appear like hunched monsters ready to pounce. All they need is someone to plug them in.

Ford sits at the table and studies the professor's old notes and lab reports. But Marla is studying something else—the knobs and switches on the grotesque and fantastic devices are what grab her attention. They might not find Wilmington's body down there, but Marla is happy. This is already more interesting than anything she has done in quite a while.

She joins Ford at the scarred table, going through the professor's notes page by page.

Hyperbolic Relativistic Projection.

Metalinear Amplitude Differentials.

It makes little sense to them, and Ford has to keep looking things up in a dictionary.

At last, with the help of the professor's notes, they're able to figure out what most of these machines are supposed to do.

The one with a metallic eyeball looking down from a tall stalk is a waterless shower that can dissolve dirt from a person's skin by <u>sonic</u> vibrations. But according to Wilmington's footnote, it doesn't work; it dissolves the skin instead of the dirt.

The device with iron tentacles growing from a steel pyramid is supposed to turn <u>molecular</u> vibrations into electricity. It works, but unfortunately it also electrocutes anyone who happens to be standing within five feet of it.

Another device—a hydrogen-powered engine—was supposed to revolutionize the automotive industry. According to a letter the professor received from the

sonic: of or relating to sound

molecular: related to molecules

PREDICT

Why did the author include this information? What will happen if Marla and Ford try to use one of the professor's machines?

chairman of one of the big car companies, the engine nearly blew up half the plant when it was turned on.

In fact, none of the things Wilmington made worked properly—not the refractive laser chain saw, or the lead-gold phase converter, or even the self-referential learning microprocessor.

"No wonder no one from the university ever came by to collect all this stuff," Marla complains. "It's all junk."

Then Marla sees the doorknob. She hadn't noticed it before because it's in a strange place—only a foot or so from the ground, half hidden behind Wilmington's nonfunctioning nuclear refrigerator.

When Ford sees it, his jaw drops with a popping sound. "A tiny door! Do you think Wilmington shrunk himself?"

"Don't be a complete gel-brain," says Marla, brushing her wild hair from her face. "It's just a root cellar. But Wilmington might be in there . . . what's left of him, anyway."

The temptation is too great. Together they push the heavy refrigerator aside, grab the knob, and swing the door wide.

An earthy smell of dry rot <u>wafts</u> out, like the smell of a grave. The door is two feet high, and inside the root cellar is pitch black. Together, Marla and Ford scramble in and vanish into darkness.

Through ancient spiderwebs they crawl until they find a dangling string. When they pull it, the room is lit by a single dim bulb that hangs from an earthen ceiling six feet from the ground.

wafts: floats through the air

There are no dead bodies down here. The smell is a sack of potatoes that have long since rotted.

But what surrounds them is enough to make their hearts miss several beats.

Razor-sharp gears, knifelike spokes, and huge magnets are frozen in position. The entire room has been converted into one big <u>contraption</u>, and in the center of it is a highbacked chair, its <u>plush</u> upholstery replaced by silver foil.

It looks like the inside of a garbage disposal, thinks Marla.

In the corner sits a pile of dusty notes, and on a control panel is an engraved silver plate that reads:

TEMPUS SYNCRO-EPICYCLUS

"What is it?" wonders Marla. She looks to Ford, whom she has already pegged to be a whiz at this scientific stuff.

Ford swallows a gulp of rotten, stale air. "I think it's a time machine."

It takes a good half hour for them to find the nerve to actually touch the thing. Ford sits on the floor most of that time, reading Wilmington's notes.

"This guy has page after page of physics formulas," Ford tells Marla. "He must have thought he was Einstein or something."

"But does it work?" she asks.

Ford furrows his brow. "I have no idea."

"There's one way to find out," she says, grabbing Ford's sweaty hand.

PREDICT

What do you think happened to Professor Wilmington? What will happen next? What details make you think as you do?

contraption: a strange machine

plush: made of thick, soft fabric

Together they run upstairs and find the perfect guinea pig: Ford's baby sister's teddy bear, Buffy. They bring Buffy down and set him on the silver chair.

"I don't know," says Ford. "Maybe we ought to know everything about this machine before we start throwing switches."

"You can't ride a bike unless you get on and pedal," says Marla, "and you can't travel through time unless you throw the switch!"

"But—"

Marla flicks the switch. The gears begin to grind, the electromagnets begin to spin and hum. They duck their heads to keep from being decapitated by the spinning spokes. Static electricity makes Ford's greased hair stand on end like Marla's. The dangling bulb dims.

There is a flash of light, and Buffy the bear is gone, leaving nothing behind but the stinging odor of <u>ozone</u> in the air. The machine grinds itself to a halt.

Ford and Marla are left gasping on the ground.

"In-totally-credible!" screeches Marla. "Now let's bring it back!"

"That's what I was trying to tell you," explains Ford, catching his breath. "According to Wilmington's journal, time travel only works one way. You can go forward in time, but you can never come back."

"That's ridiculous! That's not the way it happens in the movies."

ozone: a form of oxygen produced by electricity

"Maybe time travel doesn't work the way it does in movies," suggests Ford.

But to Marla it doesn't matter at all. The point is that however time travel works, it *does* work.

Ford looks to see where the dial is set.

"According to this," he says, "we sent the bear three days into the future. If the bear reappears in that chair three days from now, we'll really know if this thing works."

"I hate waiting," says Marla, as she impatiently picks her rhinestoned nails.

Two days later, Marla's parents read her the riot act. That is to say, they sit her down and demand she change her ways, or else.

"Your mother and I are sick and tired of you being so disrespectful," says her father.

"What's to respect?" she growls at them. "Is it my fault I was born into a family of cavepeople?"

That makes her parents boil.

"That's it," says her father. "From now on you're going to stop acting like the Queen of Mars, and you're going to start acting like a normal human being. From now on, young lady, no more neon blue lipstick. No more ultraviolet hair. No more radioactive eye shadow. No more automotive parts hanging from your earlobes. N-O-R-M-A-L. Normal! Do you understand me? Or else you get no allowance! Zero! Zilch!"

"You're so backward!" screams Marla, and she runs to her room and beats up her pillows.

Alone with her thoughts, it doesn't take her long to decide exactly what to do. Without so much as a good-bye,

PREDICT

What will Marla do now? Give reasons for your prediction.

she takes a final look at her room, then climbs out of the window and heads straight to Ford's house.

The sky is clear, filled with a million unblinking stars, and a furious wind howls through the trees. It's a perfect night for time travel.

"Marla," Ford says. "I've been reading Wilmington's notes, and there's something not quite right."

"Don't be an idiot!" Marla shouts in Ford's face. "The machine works—we saw it! We're going and that's final."

"*I'm* not going anywhere," says Ford. "I'm not into future stuff, okay?"

"It figures," huffs Marla. "I'll go by myself, then."

She pulls open the basement door and stomps down the stairs. Ford follows, trying to talk some sense into her.

"There's lots of stuff I'm still trying to figure out," he says.

"Oh, yeah?" She whirls and stares impatiently at him. "Like what?"

"Like the name of the machine," Ford says. "It bugs me. *Tempus Syncro-Epicyclus.* I looked up the word *epicyclus* in the dictionary. It has something to do with Ptolemy."

"Tommy who?" asks Marla.

"Not Tommy, *Ptolemy.* He was an ancient astronomer who believed Earth was the center of the universe, and the sun revolved around it!"

"So?" she hisses.

"So, he was wrong!" shouts Ford.

Marla shrugs. "What does that have to do with a twentieth-century genius like Wilmington? At this very moment, *he's* probably in the future, partying away, and I plan to join him."

Marla impatiently crosses the basement toward the root-cellar door.

"Marla, the last person to touch that machine must have been Wilmington—and it was set for three days! If he went three days into the future, *why didn't he come back?*"

"What are you getting at?"

"I don't know!" says Ford. "I haven't figured it out yet, but I will! Listen, at least wait until tomorrow. If the bear comes back on schedule, you can do whatever you want."

"I can't wait that long. I've got places to go!" shouts Marla.

"You're crazy!" Ford shouts back. "You're the type of person who would dive headfirst into an empty pool, just to find out how empty it is!"

Marla pulls open the root-cellar door, but Ford kicks it closed. The house rattles and moss falls from the peeling walls.

"This is my house, and that means it's my machine," he says. "I won't let you use it, so go home. Now!"

Marla turns her neon-shadowed eyes to Ford and grits her teeth. "Why you slimy little sluggardly worm-brain! How dare you tell me what I can and cannot do! You think I care what you say, you 'Leave-It-to Beaver' dweebistic troll? Marla Nixbok does what she wants, *when* she wants to do it, and if you won't throw the switch on that machine, I'll throw it myself!"

Still, Ford refuses to budge, so Marla takes her nails and heartlessly scratches his face, a maneuver she often uses when words no longer work.

PREDICT

How would you answer Ford's question? Why do you think Wilmington didn't come back?

Ford grabs his face and yelps in pain. Then he takes his foot away from the door.

"Fine," says Ford. "Go see the future. I hope you <u>materialize</u> right in the middle of a nuclear war!" With that, he storms to the stairs.

Good riddance, thinks Marla. Maybe she ought to travel fifty years into the future, just so she can find Ford as a shriveled old man and laugh in his wrinkled face.

Marla bends down and crawls into the root cellar.

At the top of the basement stairs, the truth finally strikes Buford Planct with such fury that it nearly knocks him down the stairs. If Marla uses that machine, her future won't be nuclear war. It'll be far, far from it.

"No!" he screams and races back down the stairs.

In the root cellar, Marla turns the knob to "One Year." One year is a good first trip. After that, who knows? Decades! Maybe centuries! At last she'll be free to travel to whatever time and place she feels she belongs. The Queen of Time. She likes the sound of that.

Ford crawls into the root cellar, out of breath.

"Marla, don't!" he screams.

"Get lost!" she shrieks back.

"But I figured it out!"

"Good. Does the machine work?"

"Yes, it does, but—"

"That's all I need to know!" Marla flips the switch and leaps into the silver chair. "See you next year!" she calls.

"Nooooooo!"

But Marla never gets to see the horror in Ford's eyes. Instead she sees a flash of light and is struck by a shock of

What is "the truth"? How might it be connected to Ptolemy's theory?

materialize: to appear in bodily form

Is there any way Ford could have stopped Marla? What else could he have done?

pain as she is propelled exactly one year into the future, in this, the most exciting moment of her life.

In an instant she understands it all—and it is much worse than diving into an empty pool. Now she knows what Ford had been trying so desperately to tell her, because she is now very, very cold.

And she is floating.

Ford was right: the machine works all too well. She has traveled one year forward in time.

But she isn't the center of the universe.

And neither is Earth.

Suddenly she remembers that Earth revolves around the sun, and the sun revolves around the center of the galaxy, and the galaxies are flying apart at millions of miles per hour. Everything in the universe has been moving, except for Marla Nixbok. Marla has appeared in the *exact* location in space that she had been one year ago . . .

But Earth has long since moved on.

Even the sun is gone—just one among many distant stars.

Now she knows exactly why Wilmington and Buffy the bear can never come back. And as her last breath is sucked out of her lungs by the void of space, Marla Nixbok finally gets what she has always wanted: a crystal-clear vision of her own future. Now, and forever.

The Fastest Kid Alive

Some people are so desperate they'll try just about anything—even magic.

As soon as Jim walked into the creepy old store, he knew that all the stories he had heard about it were true. All the kids knew and repeated the dark <u>speculations</u> that surrounded the old shop off Main Street, and no kid would dare go in.

It was said that black magic was sold there, and it was only because Jim was so desperate that he decided to go there. Only because he was *really* desperate.

"There's gonna be a track meet at school," he told the odd man behind the counter. "I want to be able to run faster than anyone else. I want to run so fast no one will ever be able to forget it."

"How'd you like to be the fastest kid alive?" the man asked, his eyes sparkling.

"Yeah," Jim said, "I like the sound of that—*the fastest kid alive!*"

The man went to the back of the shop and returned with a pair of wrinkled old sweat pants. He handed them to Jim, who could immediately feel a strange energy pulsing through the soft material.

speculations: guesses

"Tie the drawstring when you want to start running," the man said, "and untie it when you want to stop."

After <u>haggling</u> a bit over the price, Jim paid the man fifty dollars. He'd intended to pay only half that much, but the pants seemed worth it.

The track meet was the next day. The meet had become the most important thing in the world to Jim, because it was his last chance to prove himself at his middle school. At the end of the year, he would be graduating.

"Not Jim!" the boys would moan when he was the last player left unchosen and the teacher had to assign him to a team. "Unfair!" the chosen team would cry.

But now that he had the magic sweat pants, he was going to make everyone sorry for not wanting him on their team. Now he would leave them all in the dust. *They'll never stop talking about what happens today,* he thought. *Never!*

Jim wore the sweats out to the track loose and baggy, with the string untied like he had been warned. First, one set of five boys ran, then another. When it was Jim's turn, he stepped up to the starting line.

"On your marks!" the teacher shouted, and Jim started fumbling with the string.

"Get set!" she commanded, as Jim's trembling fingers finished tying a bow in the string.

"GO!"

Jim was off like a bullet. He was way, *way* in the lead, whizzing by the kids watching from the side of the track. He spotted the line up ahead and crossed it, grinning widely when he saw the teacher click the stopwatch with astonishment.

PREDICT

Will the pants be worth it? What might happen to make Jim sorry he's the fastest kid alive?

haggling: arguing

Then he tried to stop running . . . and tried . . . and tried. . . . But the soft cotton legs of the sweats continued to pump up and down, forcing Jim's legs to do the same.

Jim sped across the field. He could hear the kids laughing and shouting far behind him: "Go, Jim, go!" But Jim was starting to panic. He was already across the field and nearing the school buildings. Two P.E. teachers tried running after him, but there was no way they could catch up. Jim was running so fast it made them look as if they were standing still.

Then Jim remembered the old man's instruction: "Untie the pants when you want to stop."

Afraid he might run into a wall or a tree, Jim reached inside the band of the sweats and pulled the drawstring. But the loose bow he had tied at the beginning of the race had become a knot—a very *tight* knot. He tugged at it but only succeeded in making the knot tighter.

With tears forming in the corners of his eyes, Jim tried to pull the sweat pants down, but the evil pants were cinched so tightly it seemed like they would never budge.

He was out of breath now, but Jim still kept running, out the gate and down the street. There was no stopping him now, and there never would be—not the fastest kid alive.

▼ Learning from the Story

The author of "Same Time Next Year" uses dialogue
to show what the characters are like and to move the
story along. Working with a group, take turns reading
the dialogue and acting out these scenes from the story.

· Ford and Marla's meeting on the school bus
· Marla's first visit to Ford's house
· Marla's last visit to Ford's house

Discuss how dialogue makes the story more
interesting.

▼ Putting It into Practice

Develop a history for one of the main characters in
your comic book. Write a paragraph or two describing
things that happened earlier in the person's life.
Describe where he grew up or what her family was
like. What is he afraid of? Who is her best friend?
Bring in bits of your own life and the lives of people
you know.

Then give your character something to say. Write
dialogue in which the person tells about her or his
history. What the character says may or may not
match your description.

RIDING THE RAPTOR

For some people, life is one big search for the ultimate thrill—the deadlier the better.

This is gonna be great, Brent!" says my older brother, Trevor. "I can feel it."

I smile. Trevor always says that.

The trip to the top of a roller coaster always seems endless, and from up here the amusement park seems much smaller than it does from the ground. As the small train clanks its way up the steel slope of a man-made mountain, I double-check the safety bar across my lap to make sure it's tight. Then, with a mixture of terror and excitement, Trevor and I discuss how deadly that first drop is going to be. We're roller coaster fanatics, my brother and I—and this brand-new, sleek, silver beast of a ride promises to deliver ninety incredible seconds of unharnessed thrills. It's called the <u>Kamikaze</u>, and it's supposed to be the fastest, wildest roller coaster ever built. We'll see . . .

We crest the top, and everyone screams as they peer down at the dizzying drop. Then we begin to hurl downward.

Trevor puts up his hands as we pick up speed, spreading his fingers and letting the rushing wind slap against his palms. But I can never do that. Instead I grip the lap bar with sweaty palms. And I scream.

kamikaze: in World War II, a Japanese pilot who crashed a plane loaded with explosives into a ship, building, or other target

You can't help but scream at the top of your lungs on a roller coaster, and it's easy to forget everything else in the world as your body flies through the air. That feeling is special for me, but I know it's even more special for Trevor.

We reach the bottom of the first drop, and I feel myself pushed deep down into the seat as the track bottoms out and climbs once more for a loop. In an instant there is no up or down, no left or right. I feel my entire spirit become a ball of energy twisting through space at impossible speeds.

I turn my head to see Trevor. The corners of his howling mouth are turned up in a grin, and it's good to see him smile. All his bad grades, all his anger, all his fights with Mom and Dad—they're all gone when he rides the coasters. I can see it in his face. All that matters is the feel of the wind against his hands as he thrusts his fingertips into the air.

We roll one way, then the other—a double forward loop and a triple reverse <u>corkscrew</u>. The veins in my eyes bulge, my joints grind against each other, my guts climb into my throat. It's great!

One more sharp turn, and suddenly we explode back into the real world as the train returns to the station. Our car stops with a jolt, the safety bar pops up, and an anxious crowd pushes forward to take our seats.

"That was unreal!" I exclaim, my legs like rubber as we climb down the exit stairs. But Trevor is unimpressed.

"Yeah, it was okay, I guess," he says with a shrug. "But it wasn't as great as they said it would be."

I shake my head. After years of riding the rails, Trevor's become a roller coaster snob. It's been years since any coaster has delivered the particular thrill that Trevor wants.

corkscrew: a spiral route, going around and around in circles

"Well, what did you expect?" I ask him, annoyed that his lousy attitude is ruining my good time. "It's a roller coaster, not a rocket, you know?"

"Yeah, I guess," says Trevor, his disappointment growing with each step we take away from the Kamikaze. I look up and see it towering above us—all that <u>intimidating</u> silver metal. Somehow, now that we've been on it, it doesn't seem quite so intimidating.

Then I get to thinking how we waited six months for them to build it and how we waited in line for two hours to ride it, and I get even madder at Trevor for not enjoying it more.

We stop at a game on the midway, and Trevor angrily hurls baseballs at milk bottles. He's been known to throw rocks at windows with the same stone-faced anger. Sometimes I imagine my brother's soul to be like a shoelace that's all tied in an angry knot. It's a knot that only gets loose when he's riding rails at a hundred miles an hour. But as soon as the ride is over, that knot pulls itself tight again. Maybe even tighter than it was before.

Trevor furiously hurls another baseball, missing the stacked gray bottles by a mile. The guy behind the counter is a dweeb with an Adam's apple the size of a golf ball that bobs up and down when he talks. Trevor flicks him another crumpled dollar and takes aim again.

"Why don't we ride the Skull-Smasher or the Spine-Shredder," I offer. "Those aren't bad rides—and the lines aren't as long as the Kamikaze's was."

Trevor just hurls the baseball even harder, missing again. "Those are baby rides," he says with a sneer.

Why is Brent so upset with his brother?

intimidating:

threatening; frightening

"Listen, next summer we'll find a better roller coaster," I say, trying to cheer him up. "They're always building new ones."

"That's a whole year away," Trevor complains, hurling the ball again, this time nailing all three bottles at once.

The dweeb running the booth hands Trevor a purple dinosaur. "Nice shot," he grunts.

Trevor looks at the purple thing with practiced disgust.

Great, I think. *Trevor's already bored out of his mind, and it's only this amusement park's opening day.* As I watch my brother, I know what'll happen now; five more minutes, and he'll start finding things to do that will get us into trouble, deep trouble. It's how Trevor is.

That's when I catch sight of the tickets thumbtacked to the booth's wall, right alongside the row of purple dinosaurs—two tickets with red printing on gold paper.

"What are those?" I ask the dweeb running the booth.

"Beats me," he says, totally clueless. "You want 'em instead of the dinosaur?"

We make the trade, and I read the tickets as we walk away: GOOD FOR ONE RIDE ON THE RAPTOR.

"What's the Raptor?" I ask Trevor.

"Who knows," he says. "Probably some dumb kiddie-go-round thing, like everything else in this stupid place."

I look on the amusement park map but can't find the ride anywhere. Then, through the opening-day crowds, I look up and see a hand-painted sign that reads THE RAPTOR in big red letters. The sign is pointing down toward a path that no one else seems to be taking. That alone is enough to catch Trevor's interest, as well as mine.

raptor: a bird of prey, such as an eagle or a hawk

He glances around <u>furtively</u>, as if he's about to do something he shouldn't, then says, "Let's check it out."

He leads the way down the path, and as always, I follow.

The dark asphalt we are on leads down into thick bushes, and the sounds of the amusement park crowd get farther and farther away, until we can't hear them at all.

"I think we made a wrong turn," I tell Trevor, studying the map, trying to get my bearings. Then suddenly a deep voice booms in the bushes beside us.

"You're looking for the Raptor, are you?"

We turn to see a clean-shaven man dressed in the gray-and-blue uniform that all the ride operators wear, only his doesn't seem to be made of the same awful polyester. Instead his uniform shimmers like satin. So do his eyes, blue-gray eyes that you can't look into, no matter how hard you try.

I look at Trevor, and tough as he is, he can't look the man in the face.

"The name's DelRio," the man says. "I run the Raptor."

"What is the Raptor?" asks Trevor.

DelRio grins. "You mean you don't know?" He reaches out his long fingers and pulls aside the limbs of a dense thornbush. "There you are, gentlemen—the Raptor!"

What we see doesn't register at first. When something is so big—so indescribably huge—sometimes your brain can't quite wrap around it. All you can do is blink and stare, trying to force your mind to accept what it sees.

There's a valley before us, and down in the valley is a wooden roller coaster painted black as night. But the amazing thing is that the valley itself is part of the roller

furtively: secretly; sneakily

coaster. Its peaks rise on either side of us in a tangle of tracks that stretch off in all directions as if there is nothing else but the Raptor from here to the ends of the earth.

"No way," Trevor gasps, more impressed than I've ever seen him. "This must be the biggest roller coaster in the world!"

"The biggest *anywhere*," corrects DelRio.

In front of us is the ride's platform with sleek red cars, ready to go.

"Something's wrong," I say, although I can't quite figure out what it is. "Why isn't this ride on the map?"

"New attraction," says DelRio.

"So how come there's no crowd?" asks Trevor.

DelRio smiles and looks through us with those awful eyes. "The Raptor is by invitation only." He takes our tickets, flipping them over to read the back. "Trevor and Brent Collins," he says. "Pleased to have you aboard."

Trevor and I look at each other, then at the torn ticket stubs DelRio has just handed back to us. Sure enough, our names are printed right there on the back, big as life.

"Wait! How did—" But before I can ask, Trevor cuts me off, his eyes already racing along the wildly twisting tracks of the gigantic contraption.

"That first drop," he says, "that's three hundred feet."

"Oh, the first drop's grand!" DelRio exclaims. "But on this ride, it's the last drop that's special."

I can see Trevor licking his lips, losing himself in the sight of the amazing ride. It's good to see him excited like this . . . and *not* good, too.

Name some words and phrases that describe what DelRio looks like. What words and phrases describe the roller coaster?

Every time DelRio talks, I get a churning feeling in my gut—the kind of feeling you get when you find half a worm in your apple. Still, I can't figure out what's wrong.

"Are we the only ones invited?" I ask <u>tentatively</u>.

DelRio smiles. "Here come the others now."

I turn to see a group of gawking kids coming through the bushes, and DelRio greets them happily. The look in their eyes is exactly like Trevor's. They don't just want to ride the coaster—they *need* to ride it.

"Since you're the first, you can ride in the front," DelRio tells us. "Aren't you the lucky ones!"

While Trevor psyches himself up for the ride and while DelRio tears tickets, I slip away into the <u>superstructure</u> of the great wooden beast. I'm searching for something— although I'm not sure what it is. I follow the track with my eyes, but it's almost impossible to stick with it. It twists and spins and loops in ways that wooden roller coasters aren't supposed to be able to do—up and down, back and forth, until my head gets dizzy and little squirmy spots appear before my eyes. It's like a huge angry knot.

Before long I'm lost in the immense web of wood, but still I follow the path of the rails with my eyes until I come to that last drop that DelRio claimed was so special. I follow its long path up . . . and then down . . .

In an instant I understand just what it is about this ride I couldn't put my finger on before. Now I *know* I have to stop Trevor from getting on it.

In a wild panic I race back through the dark wooden frame of the Raptor, dodging low-hanging beams that poke out at odd angles.

tentatively: uncertainly; hesitantly

superstructure: the rails, ties, and support beams of a roller coaster

PREDICT

What might Brent have found out? Will he be able to stop Trevor from riding the Raptor? Why do you think as you do?

When I finally reach the platform, everyone is sitting in the cars, ready to go. The only empty seat is in the front car. It's the seat beside Trevor. DelRio waits impatiently by a big lever extending from the ground.

"Hurry, Brent," DelRio says, scowling. "Everyone's waiting."

"Yes! Yes!" shout all the kids. "Hurry! Hurry! We want to RIDE!"

They start cheering for me to get in, to join my brother in the front car. But I'm frozen on the platform.

"Trevor!" I finally manage to say, gasping for breath. "Trevor, you have to get off that ride."

"What are you, nuts?" he shouts.

"We can't ride this coaster!" I insist.

Trevor ignores me, fixing his gaze straight ahead. But that's not the direction in which he should be looking. He should be looking at the track behind the last car— because if he does, he'll see that there is no track behind the last car!

"The coaster doesn't come back!" I shout at him. "Don't you see? It doesn't come back!"

Trevor finally turns to me, his hands shaking in <u>infinite</u> terror and ultimate excitement . . . and then he says . . .

"I know."

I take a step back.

I can't answer that. I can't accept it. I need more time, but everyone is shouting at me to get on the ride, and DelRio is getting more and more impatient. That's when Trevor reaches out his hand toward me, his fingers bone white, trembling with anticipation.

infinite: great; extreme

"Ride with me, Brent," he pleads desperately. "It'll be great. I can feel it!"

I reach out my hand. My fingers are an inch from his.

"Please . . ." Trevor pleads.

He's my brother. He wants me to go. They *all* want me to go. What could be better than riding in the front car, twisting through all those spins and drops? I can see it now: Trevor and me—the way it's always been—his hands high in the air, wrestling the wind, and me gripping the safety bar.

Only thing is, the Raptor *has* no safety bar.

I pull my hand back away from his. *I won't follow you, Trevor!* my mind screams. *Not today. Not ever again.*

When Trevor sees me backing away, his face hardens— the way it hardens toward our parents or his teachers or anyone else who's on the outside of his closed world. "Wimp!" he shouts at me. "*Loooooser!*"

DelRio tightly grips the lever. "This isn't a ride for the weak," he says, his hawk eyes judging me, trying to make me feel small and useless. "Stand back and let the big kids ride."

He pulls back on the lever, and slowly the Raptor slides forward, catching on a heavy chain that begins to haul it up to the first big drop. Trevor has already turned away from me, locking his eyes on the track rising before him, preparing himself for the thrill of his life.

The coaster clacketty-clacks all the way to the top. Then the red train begins to fall, its metal wheels throwing sparks and screeching all the way down. All I can do is watch as Trevor puts up his hands and rides. The wooden beast of a roller coaster groans and roars like a dragon, and

If you were Brent, would you get on the ride? Why or why not?

the tiny red train rockets deep inside the black wooden framework stretching to the horizon.

Up and down, back and forth, the Raptor races. Time is paralyzed as its trainload of riders rockets through thrill after terrifying thrill, until finally, after what seems like an eternity, it reaches that last mountain.

DelRio turns to me. "The grand finale," he announces. "You could have been there—*you* could have had the ultimate thrill if you weren't a coward, Brent."

But I know better. This time, *I* am the brave one.

The red train climbs the final peak, defying gravity, moving up and up until it's nothing more than a tiny red sliver against a blue sky . . . and then it begins the trip down, accelerating faster than gravity can pull it. It's as if the ground itself were sucking it down from the clouds.

The Raptor's whole wooden framework rumbles like an earthquake. I hold on to a black beam, and I feel my teeth rattle in my head. I want to close my eyes, but I keep them open, watching every last second.

I can see Trevor alone in the front car. His hands are high, slapping <u>defiantly</u> against the wind, and he's screaming louder than all the others as the train <u>plummets</u> straight down . . . into that awful destiny that awaits it.

I can see that destiny from here now, looming larger than life—a bottomless, blacker-than-black pit.

I watch as my brother and all the others are pulled from the sky, down into that emptiness . . . and then they are swallowed by it, their thrilled screams silenced without so much as an echo.

The ride is over.

To what does the author compare the Raptor?

defiantly: openly resisting

plummets: drops; plunges

I am horrified, but DelRio remains unmoved. He casually glances at his watch, then turns and shouts deep into the superstructure of the roller coaster. "Time!"

All at once hundreds of workers crawl from the woodwork like ants. Nameless, faceless people, each with some kind of tool like a hammer or wrench practically growing from their arms. They all set upon the Raptor, dismantling it with incredible speed.

"What is this?" I ask DelRio. "What's going on?"

"Surely you don't expect an attraction this special to stay in one place?" he <u>scoffs</u>. "We must travel! There are worlds of people waiting for the thrill of a lifetime!"

When I look again at the roller coaster, it's gone. Nothing remains but the workers carrying its heavy beams off through the thick underbrush.

DelRio smiles at me. "We'll see you again, Brent," he says. "Perhaps next time you'll ride."

As the last of the workers carry away the final rail of the Raptor on their horribly hunched backs, I stare DelRio down. I can look him in the eyes now, unflinching.

"Tell your friends about the Raptor," he says, then he pauses and adds, "No . . . on second thought, don't tell them a thing. Wouldn't want to spoil their surprise."

Then he strolls after the workers, who are carrying the Raptor to its next location. I just stand there.

No, I won't tell anyone—ever. What could I possibly say? And if I encounter the Raptor again someday, I can only hope I will have the strength to stare DelRio down once more, dig my heels deep into the earth beneath my feet . . . and refuse to ride.

scoffs: makes fun of; mocks

RIDING THE RAPTOR

▼ Learning from the Story

"Riding the Raptor" describes several rides and a midway in an amusement park. Can you visualize the setting? Working with several other students, draw a map of this amusement park. Sketch in all the rides and the game booth described in the story and add a few more. Don't forget to include the Raptor.

Compare your map with maps created by other groups. Notice how differently people visualized the same setting, based on their own experiences and imaginations.

▼ Putting It into Practice

Think about where your "wishful" story will take place—a big city, your own town, a deserted house. Maybe your story has more than one setting. Visualize one of the settings. Follow these steps to make your setting come to life.

1. Freewrite about what the place is like and what mood you want to create.
2. Make a shoebox set of the place.
3. Paint or paper the inside walls of the box.
4. Add magazine cutouts of furniture and other items.

Your shoebox set will help you or your comic book artist see exactly what you have in mind.

TRASH DAY

Sometimes it's hard to know what to get rid of—and when to get rid of it.

It began long before that *thing* arrived on their lawn.

In fact, it began long before Lucinda Pudlinger was born. There was no way to know all the strange and mysterious forces that had created the Pudlinger family. Nevertheless, all those forces bubbled and brewed together and spat out the Pudlingers on the doormat of humanity.

As for Lucinda, it had never really occurred to her how serious her situation was until the day Garson McCall walked her home from school.

"You really don't have to," Lucinda had told him, more as a warning than anything else. Still, Garson had insisted. For reasons that Lucinda could not understand, he had a crush on her.

"No," said Garson, "I really want to walk you home."

Lucinda didn't mind the attention, but she did mind the fact that Garson was going to meet her family. There was no preparing him for *that*.

As they rounded the corner on that autumn afternoon, the Pudlinger home came into view. It was halfway down a street of identical tract homes—but there was nothing about where the Pudlingers lived that matched the other homes.

True, they had a small front lawn like every other house on the block, but on the Pudlingers' lawn there were three rusting cars with no wheels—and a fourth piled on top of the other three. The four useless vehicles had been there, as far as Lucinda knew, since the beginning of time. While others might keep such old wrecks with an eye toward restoring them, the Pudlingers, it seemed, just collected them.

There was also a washing machine on that lawn. It didn't work, but Lucinda's mom had filled it with barbecue ashes and turned it into a planter. Of course, only weeds would grow in it, but then weeds were Mrs. Pudlinger's specialty. One only needed to look at the rest of the yard to see that.

As for the house itself, the roof shingles looked like a jigsaw puzzle minus a number of pieces, and the pea-green aluminum siding was peeling (which was something aluminum siding wasn't supposed to do).

The Pudlinger place didn't just draw your attention when you walked by it. No, it grabbed your eyeballs and dragged them kicking and screaming out of their sockets. In fact, if you looked up _eyesore_ in the dictionary, Lucinda was convinced it would say "See Pudlinger."

"Look at that place!" said Garson as they walked down the street. "Is that a house or the city dump?"

"It's _my_ house," said Lucinda, figuring the truth was less painful when delivered quickly.

"Oh," replied Garson, his face turning red from the foot he had just put into his mouth. "I didn't mean there

eyesore: something offensive to look at

was anything *wrong* with it—it just looks . . . lived-in. Yeah, that's right—lived-in . . . in a homey sort of way."

"Homely" is more like it, thought Lucinda.

Out front there was a fifth rusty auto relic that still worked, parked by the curb. A pair of legs attached to black boots stuck out from underneath. As Garson and Lucinda approached, a boy of about fifteen crawled out from under the car, stood in their path, and flexed his muscles in a threatening way. He wore a black T-shirt that said DIE, and he had dirty-blond hair with streaks of age-old grease in it. His right arm was substantially more muscular than his left, the way crabs often have one claw much bigger than the other.

"Who's this dweeb?" the filthy teenager said through a mouth full of teeth, none of which seemed to be growing in the same direction. He looked Garson up and down.

Lucinda sighed. "Garson, this is my brother, Ignatius."

"My friends call me 'Itchy,'" (which didn't mean much, since Ignatius had no friends). "You ain't a nerd, are you?" Itchy asked the boy standing uncomfortably next to Lucinda.

"No, not recently," Garson replied.

"Good. I hate nerds." And with that, Itchy reached out his muscular right arm and shook Garson's hand, practically shattering Garson's finger bones. It was <u>intentional</u>.

"Hey, wanna help me chase the neighborhood cats into traffic?" Itchy asked. "It's a blast!"

"No thanks," said Garson. "I'm allergic to cats."

Itchy shrugged. "Your loss," he said, then returned to tormenting the fat tabby that was hiding under the car.

intentional: done on purpose

"What's with him?" asked Garson as he and Lucinda made their way toward the house.

Lucinda rolled her eyes. "He's been bored ever since he got expelled."

What Lucinda neglected to say was how happy her brother was to be out of school. He'd planned on getting out ever since last summer when he'd gotten a job operating the Tilt-A-Whirl at the local carnival. It was that job which had given him his powerful right arm. Pull the lever, push the lever, press the button—if he worked at it hard enough, and practiced at home, Itchy was convinced operating the Tilt-A-Whirl could become a full-time career. With a future that bright, who needed school?

"Lucinda!" shouted Itchy, still under the car. "Mom and Dad are looking for you . . . and they're mad."

Lucinda shrugged. That was no news. They were always that way.

She turned to Garson. "You don't have to come in," she said, more in warning than anything else.

But Garson forced a smile. He was going to see this through to the end, no matter how horrible that end might be. And it was.

The inside of the Pudlinger home was no more inviting than the outside. It had curling wallpaper, brown carpet that had clearly started out as a different color, and faded furniture that would cause any respectable interior decorator to jump off a cliff.

Mr. Pudlinger was in his usual position on the recliner, with a beer in his hand, releasing belches of unusual

PREDICT

How will Garson's visit turn out? What makes you think as you do?

<u>magnitude</u>. He stared at a TV with the colors set so peoples' faces were purple and their hair was green.

"Where have you been?" he growled at Lucinda.

"Field hockey practice," she answered flatly.

"You didn't take out the trash this morning," he said, grunting.

"Yes, I did."

"Then how come it's full again?"

Lucinda glanced over to see that the trash can was indeed full—full of the usual fast-food wrappers, beer cans, and unpaid bills.

"You take that trash out before dark, or no allowance!" her dad yelled from across the room. It must have slipped his mind that Lucinda didn't get an allowance. Not that they couldn't afford it—they weren't poor. It was just that her mom and dad liked to "put money away for a rainy day." Obviously they thought there was a drought.

Mr. Pudlinger shifted in his recliner, and it let out a frightened squeak the way recliners do when holding someone of exceptional weight. It wasn't that Lucinda's dad was fat. It would have been perfectly all right if he was *just* fat. But the truth was, he was also . . . misshapen. He had a hefty beer gut, and somehow that beer gut had settled into strange, unexpected regions of his body, until he looked like some horrible reflection in a fun-house mirror.

"What does your father *do*?" Garson asked as they stepped over the living room debris toward the kitchen.

"What he's doing right now," she replied. "That's what he does."

magnitude: great size or extent

"No, I mean for a living," Garson clarified.

"Like I said, *that's* what he does." Lucinda then went on to explain how her father was hurt on the job six years ago and how he had been home ever since, receiving disability pay from the government. "He calls it 'living off of Uncle Sam,'" said Lucinda. Of course, Mr. Pudlinger failed to tell Uncle Sam that he had completely recovered two weeks after the accident.

In the kitchen they ran into Lucinda's mom, whom Lucinda had also wanted to avoid. The woman had a cigarette permanently fixed to a scowl that was permanently planted on her mouth, which was permanently painted with more lipstick than Bozo the Clown.

Lucinda reluctantly introduced her to Garson.

"Garson?" she said through her frowning clown lips. "What kind of stupid name is that?" Cough, cough.

"I'm named after my father," Garson replied.

"Yeah, yeah, whatever," she said and spat her gum into the sink, where it caught on the lip of a dirty glass. "You wanna stay for dinner, Garson?" she asked, batting her eyes, showing off those caterpillarlike things she glued to her lashes.

"What are you having?" he asked.

"Leftovers," she said flatly.

Garson grimaced. "Left over from what?"

Mrs. Pudlinger was stumped by that one. No one had ever asked that before. "Just leftovers," she said. "You know, like from the refrigerator."

"No, thanks," said Garson. Clearly, his survival instinct had kicked in.

PREDICT

What does the author mean when he says that Garson's survival instinct had kicked in?

Lucinda watched tearfully as, moments later, Garson walked down the street, having hastily said goodbye to her horrible family. It was the last straw, the last time she would allow her family to humiliate her like this. Their reign of terror had to end.

Just as she turned to go back into the house, a car swerved in the street, its tires screeching as it tried to avoid a cat. The cat, having just missed being flattened, leaped into the arms of an elderly neighbor woman across the street. She turned a clouded eye at Itchy, who had just climbed out from under a parked car, laughing.

"You monster!" the old woman screamed, shaking her cane at him. "You horrible, evil boy!"

"Ah, shut yer trap, you old bat," Itchy snarled.

"You're trash!" the old woman shouted. "Every last one of you Pudlingers. The way you keep your house—the way you live your lives—*you're all trash!*"

That's when Mr. Pudlinger came out onto the porch. It was the first time Lucinda had seen him outside in months. He turned to Itchy, put a hand on the boy's shoulder, and as if speaking words of <u>profound</u> wisdom, said, "Don't let anyone who's not family call you trash."

And then he went across the street and punched the old lady out.

When Lucinda's <u>salvation</u> finally came, it came thundering out of nowhere at five in the morning. That's when a mighty crash shook the house like an earthquake, waking everyone up.

profound: showing great understanding or knowledge

salvation: deliverance from evil or difficulty

How does Lucinda feel about her family? Complete this statement for Lucinda: "I wish . . ."

Furious to have been shaken awake, Mr. Pudlinger shuffled out of the bedroom with Mrs. Pudlinger close behind, her face caked in some sort of green beauty mud that actually looked less <u>offensive</u> than her regular face.

"What's going on around here?" bellowed Mr. Pudlinger. "Can't a man get any sleep?"

Lucinda wandered out of her bedroom, and Itchy—a true coward when it came to anything other than cats and nerds—came out of his bedroom and hid behind her.

Together the family shuffled to the front door and opened it to find yet another object on their front lawn— a Dumpster.

Dark green, with heavy ridges all around it, the huge metal trash container was one of those large ones used in construction—eight feet high and twenty feet long. Yet it seemed like no Dumpster Lucinda had ever seen before.

"Cool," said Itchy, who must have already been calculating a hundred awful ways the thing could be used.

Mr. Pudlinger scratched his flaking scalp. "Who sent a Dumpster to us?" he asked.

"Maybe the Home Shopping Network," suggested Itchy.

"Naah," said Mom. "I didn't order a Dumpster."

But it clearly was meant for them, because the name "Pudlinger" was stenciled on the side.

It's like a puzzle, thought Lucinda. *What's wrong with this picture?*

But there were already so many things wrong with the Pudlinger lawn that the Dumpster just blended right in. Slowly Lucinda went up to it. It looked so . . . heavy. More

offensive: disgusting; unpleasant

than heavy, it looked dense. She looked down to see a tiny hint of metal sticking out from underneath. The edge of a car muffler poked out like the wicked witch's feet from beneath Dorothy's house.

Mrs. Pudlinger gasped. "Look!" she said. "It crushed the Volkswagen Itchy was born in!"

Mr. Pudlinger began to fume. "I'll sue!" he shouted. And with that he stormed back into the house and began to flip through the Yellow Pages in search of a lawyer.

The Dumpster caught the sun and cast a dark shadow. As Lucinda left for school that day, she couldn't help but stare at the thing as she walked around it to get to the street.

It's just a Dumpster, she tried to tell herself. The way she figured it, some neighbor—some *angry* neighbor— took it upon himself to provide a container large enough to haul away all the junk her family had <u>accumulated</u> over the years. But if that were so, then why didn't they hear the truck that brought it here?

Before Lucinda knew what she was doing, she had put down her books and was walking toward the gigantic green container. Slowly she began to touch it, brushing her fingers across the metal, then laying her hand flat against its cold, smooth surface. As she touched it, all thoughts seemed to empty from her mind. It was as if the Dumpster was hypnotizing her. She giggled to herself for thinking such a silly thought and stepped away from the huge bin.

Then the Dumpster shifted just a bit, and the dead Volkswagen Bug beneath it creaked a flat complaint.

PREDICT

Where do you think the Dumpster came from? How will it change the Pudlingers' lives?

accumulated: collected little by little

Anything that crushes one of our lawn cars can't be all bad, thought Lucinda with a chuckle.

No, Lucinda decided, this thing was not evil—far from it. In fact, to Lucinda it seemed almost . . . friendly—certainly more friendly than anything else on their poor excuse for a lawn. And, clearly, it seemed to be waiting. Yes, happily waiting for something . . . but what?

Whistling to herself, Lucinda turned away. And as she strolled off to school, she thought about the great green metal box and the way it sat in anticipation, like a Christmas present waiting to be opened.

The neighbor's fat tabby cat was sitting proudly on the hood of one of the lawn cars when Lucinda returned home that afternoon. The Dumpster hadn't moved.

All day Lucinda hadn't been able to get it out of her mind. It was as if the thing had fallen into her brain instead of onto their weed-choked lawn. In fact, she had actually looked forward to coming home, just so she could take a good look at it again. There was something noble about the way it stood there—like a silent <u>monolith</u>.

But it isn't silent, is it? Lucinda thought. There were noises coming from within its dark-green depths—little scratches and creaks, like rats crawling around. *Is there something alive in there?* she wondered. *Is there anything in there at all, or is it just my imagination?*

If it had been a Christmas present, Lucinda would have been able to shake it, feel its weight, and try to guess what it held. But there was no way she could lift a Dumpster.

monolith: a monument made from one large block of stone

Unable to stand not knowing what was inside, she ran to the porch and got several chairs and stacked them one on top of the other. Then she climbed the rickety tower she had created and peered over the edge of the Dumpster.

As she had expected, it wasn't empty, and the shock of what Lucinda saw nearly made her lose her balance and tumble back to the ground. But she held on, refusing to blink as she stared down into the Dumpster . . .

. . . at her father, who sat in his recliner, watching TV.

"Dad?" she shouted. "Dad, what are you doing?"

"What does it look like I'm doing?" he asked, clicking the remote control with the speed of a semiautomatic weapon. "Get me the TV program guide, or you're grounded!"

In another corner of the Dumpster sat Lucinda's mother, with her entire vanity and makeup collection before her. She scowled at her own reflection, took a deep drag of her cigarette, and began to apply a fresh layer of makeup.

"Mom?"

"Leave me alone," she said. "I'm having a bad hair day." Cough, cough.

In the third corner of the Dumpster stood Itchy. There was a lever coming from the metal floor, and a button on the wall. Pull the lever, push the lever, press the button. Pull the lever, push the lever, press the button—Itchy was working away.

"Have you all gone crazy?" yelled Lucinda. "Don't you know where you are?"

But it was clear that they didn't. Her father thought he was in the living room, her mother thought she was in the bedroom, and Itchy, well, he thought he was king of the Tilt-A-Whirl. They all were in their own private little heaven, if you could call it that. This Dumpster—this terrible, wonderful Dumpster—wasn't designed to haul away *things*—it was designed to haul away *people*!

"Well, are you coming inside or what?" asked her father.

Should Lucinda join her family? Would you? Why or why not?

Lucinda could have argued with them. And maybe, if she tried hard enough, she could have broken through their little <u>trances</u> and made them come out.

But if she tried hard enough, she could also keep herself from telling them anything at all.

That thought brought the tiniest grin to her face—a grin that widened as she leaped to the ground, into a tangle of weeds that cushioned her fall. Her smile continued to grow as she stepped into the house, and she broke into a full-fledged laughing fit as she raced into her room and began to bounce on her bed.

The Dumpster was taken away sometime during the night.

PREDICT

What will Lucinda's life be like now?

The following week, Garson McCall stopped by to apologize for being so rude on his first visit. The startled look on his face didn't surprise Lucinda. She had many startled visitors during those first few days. One need only look at the carless, freshly planted lawn to know something had changed.

trances: dazed conditions

"Hi, Garson," said Lucinda in a dark, sad tone that didn't seem to match the brightness of the spotless house.

"Wow! What an overhaul!" exclaimed Garson as he stepped inside, his eyes bugging out at the new carpet and furniture.

Lucinda just shrugged.

A fifteen-year-old kid came bounding out of the kitchen to greet him, wearing a million-dollar smile that showed perfect teeth. "Hi, Garson, what's up?" the boy asked.

"Itchy?" Garson murmured in disbelief.

"Ignatius," the clean-cut boy corrected. "But my friends call me Nate."

In the living room a man who looked like an athletic version of Mr. Pudlinger was sipping lemonade and reading *Parents* magazine. In the kitchen a woman who resembled Mrs. Pudlinger, with several coats of makeup peeled away, was baking a pie.

"Garson, would you like to stay for dinner?" asked the pleasant-looking woman. "We're having T-bone steak and apple pie!"

"Sure," said Garson.

Lucinda could practically see him drool, but the flat expression on her own face never changed. In fact, she didn't know if she *could* change it anymore.

"I can't believe these are the same people I saw last week!" whispered Garson excitedly.

"They're not," said Lucinda. "They're replacements sent by the Customer Service Department."

Garson laughed, as if Lucinda had made a joke, and Lucinda didn't have the strength to convince him it was true.

Lucinda got her wish. Why isn't she happy with her new, improved family?

"Listen, Garson," she finally said. "I'd like to talk, but I can't. I have to study."

"Study?" Garson raised an eyebrow. "On a Saturday?"

"I have to get an A in math," Lucinda replied.

"And science," added the new Mrs. Pudlinger cheerfully.

"Don't forget English and history," Mr. Pudlinger sang out. "My daughter's going to be a straight-A student, just like her brother!"

Lucinda sighed, feeling herself go weak at the knees. "*And* I have to be the star of the field hockey team. *And* I have to keep my room spotlessly clean. *And* I have to do all my chores *perfectly* . . . or else."

"Or else . . . what?" asked Garson.

Then Lucinda leaned in close, and with panic in her eyes, she desperately whispered in his ear, "Or else it comes back for me!"

Mrs. Pudlinger turned from her perfect pie. "Lucinda, dear," she said with a smile that seemed just a bit too wide, "isn't it your turn to take out the garbage?"

"Yes, Mother," Lucinda replied woodenly.

Then Lucinda Pudlinger, dragging her feet across the floor like a zombie, took out the trash . . . being *horribly* careful not to let a single scrap of paper fall to the ground. Ever.

▼ Learning from the Story

The author of "Trash Day" includes vivid descriptions that help the reader picture characters and settings. Work with a partner to complete a Before and After comparison chart for a character or setting from the story. Include details such as what a place looked like, how people acted, and what they said. After your chart is completed, refer to it to help you draw Before and After pictures. Compare your chart and pictures with those of other groups in your class.

▼ Putting It into Practice

Comic book stories don't have many words. The words that you use should be vivid and descriptive. Read over your comic book script. Replace any boring words with words that leap off the page. Use vivid words to give your characters unique personalities. Don't forget, in comics you can also single out vivid words and sounds and picture them as part of the art.

Last Minute

Have you ever wished that you had more hours in a day? more days in a week? more weeks in a year?

M olly Strong's clock radio alarm went off suddenly on her night table, awakening her from a deep, dreamless sleep. *It can't be time to get up already!* she thought in her sleep-fogged brain. *Can it?*

The eighth grader yawned and slipped on her bathrobe. She couldn't remember how late she had stayed up finishing her science report. *Was it 1:00 or 2:00 A.M.?* she wondered, as she plodded down the cold hallway of the drafty old house, silently scolding herself for waiting, once again, until the last minute to do her homework.

She'd been given the assignment weeks ago, but true to the nickname her father had given her—Miss <u>Molasses</u>— Molly just couldn't motivate herself to get started. Now she would drag around school all day like a zombie. "Oh, well," she grumbled, as she shuffled into the kitchen. "At least I finished the stupid report. Better late than never."

Grabbing some milk from the refrigerator and some cereal from the pantry, Molly settled down in the breakfast nook to eat. As she did, she looked out at the gray

molasses: a sweet, thick syrup that flows very slowly

morning. Raindrops were zigging and zagging down the bay window that overlooked the cove. It had poured almost every day since her family had moved to northwest Washington from southern California. Feeling a little depressed, Molly thought about all her old friends, and as she chewed her soggy cornflakes, she longed for the carefree days she used to spend with them, hanging out at the mall or soaking up the sun at the beach.

Life sure had changed since her father had gotten that promotion and her mother had <u>passed the bar</u>. Now everyone—everyone but her—seemed to be in a rush. Her father was off to work at his computer company at the crack of dawn. Her mother was out the door to her law office a few minutes later. Even Steve, her brother, had already flown out of the house. He was now a big high school senior and rode to school with a few of his new buddies who had cars.

Finishing her cereal, Molly got up to wash out her bowl. There, hanging over the sink, was Captain Bradley's clock, shaped like the wheel of an old sailing boat. The clock was one of many <u>mementos</u> from all the exotic ports the old <u>merchant marine</u> had visited. Molly's mother had found it in a beaten-up trunk left behind by Bradley's daughters when they had sold the house to the Strongs after their father's death at the age of ninety-seven. In their early seventies themselves, Claudia and Harriet Bradley were apparently in such a hurry to leave the overcast and chilly Northwest that they not only left the old trunk behind, but also forgot to leave a forwarding address.

What are some reasons why Molly is feeling "a little depressed"?

passed the bar: passed a test to become a lawyer

mementos: keepsakes or souvenirs that are reminders of the past

merchant marine: a sailor who works on a ship that carries goods to sell to other countries

Molly was fascinated by all the stuff in Captain Bradley's trunk and loved the way the old clock gave the kitchen a <u>nautical</u> feel. As she absentmindedly gazed up at it now, she thought of all the interesting places the old sailor must have seen and all the experiences he must have had. But then she felt Donald, her old tabby cat, rub against her leg and suddenly realized that if she daydreamed any longer, she'd miss the bus.

Why, oh, why can't I get a grip on time? she wondered, exasperated with herself as she threw on her clothes, ran a comb through her hair, brushed her teeth, and flew out the door . . . just as the school bus roared away.

It was three days later when Molly's problem with time hit her again. She was sitting in the back of her last-period social studies class, frantically trying to finish the essay section of a big test.

"Hurry up, people," Mr. Rand said, as he checked his watch. "You have three minutes until the bell. Those of you who've already finished can get a head start on tomorrow's reading assignment."

Molly wrote as fast as she could, but she had a hard time getting her thoughts on paper. She felt so rushed, just like she always did. The questions were hard, and she wished now that she'd reviewed the chapter more carefully. Of course, she'd known about the test for a week, but that didn't mean anything to her. As she did with everything in her life, Molly had waited until the last minute to read the material, and now she was paying for it.

nautical: having to do with ships and sailors

The bell rang and the room exploded into a flurry of kids crowding for the door. Molly, feeling very upset with herself, was not one of them. Instead, she dragged herself from behind her desk, made her way slowly over to Mr. Rand, and, with her head down, handed him her test—only three-quarters finished.

"Not enough time, Molly?" Mr. Rand asked as he hurriedly tossed her test into his briefcase.

"Never enough time, Mr. Rand," Molly answered with a shrug. "I don't know why, but time always seems to get away from me."

Mr. Rand snapped his briefcase shut and looked over his glasses at her. "Sounds like you just have to learn to manage your schedule a little better," the gray-haired man said encouragingly. "<u>Prioritize</u> everything you have to do and don't save things until the last minute."

Molly nodded as she walked slowly behind Mr. Rand down the hall. She knew that waiting until the last minute was her biggest problem. She had to play it smarter, to plan ahead. *No more wasting time,* she thought as she collected her books from her locker. *From now on I'm going to grab hold of time and make the most of it!*

But a week later, Molly was caught in yet another time predicament. Sitting slumped at her desk, she looked out at the rain drumming furiously against her bedroom window. It was already 10:30 at night and she still had a three-page book report on Charles Dickens's *Great Expectations* to write. She'd known about it for several weeks, but it had taken her that long just to read the book.

prioritize: to put in order of importance

Looking away from the dreary rain, Molly was just starting to get back to work when she noticed her mother standing in the doorway.

"Why are you still up?" her mother asked. "You're going to be exhausted in the morning if you don't get some rest, honey."

Molly shrugged. "I can't go to bed yet, Mom," she said. "I still have a book report to write. It's due tomorrow."

Her mother raised her eyebrows. "A book report? Why did you save something like that for the last minute?" she asked sternly.

"It really doesn't matter what I do, Mom," Molly muttered. "Something *always* ends up getting left until the last minute."

Her mother shook her head wearily as she turned away. "I don't know about you, Miss Molasses," she said, as she walked down the narrow hallway to her bedroom where Molly's dad was already snoring loudly. "Make sure you put the cat down in the basement and change the litter before you turn in, will you, honey?"

"Sure, Mom," Molly said, giving the big tabby, now curled up on her desk, an affectionate scratch behind the ears. "I'll take care of Donald."

Looking at her with his big green eyes, Donald purred loudly as Molly turned back to her computer, once again prepared to begin the late-night drudgery of her book report. But before she'd typed the first word, an icy gust of wind wailed against the window, sending a draft under the old sill.

"Brrrr," Molly said, shuddering.

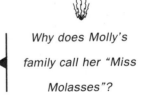

Why does Molly's family call her "Miss Molasses"?

She padded over to the <u>cubbyhole</u> closet behind her bed, slid open the dark wood panel, and yanked a big knitted <u>afghan</u> from the pile of bedding her mother kept there. As the afghan unfurled, Molly heard something clatter to the floor. "Hmm, what's this?" she muttered, picking up a small wooden box about the size of a thick paperback book.

She blew off the dust covering it, then took the box over to her desk for a better look. There was strange writing on the lid in a language that Molly had never seen before. Even though she didn't know the language, something about the twisted, <u>curlicue</u> letters made them seem like some kind of warning.

"I wonder what's in here," Molly said softly as she pried open the strange-looking box and peered inside.

There, sitting on a velvet cushion, was the most incredible watch she had ever seen. Its band was made of two parallel rows of jade and silver oval beads, its face was emerald colored with small gold dots that marked off the hours, and its hands were intricately carved and made of polished black metal.

"Whoaaa," Molly gasped, as she gently lifted the timepiece from its velvet pad. "This watch is incredible." She turned its tiny stem around in one complete clockwise circle, then held the watch to her ear. *Tick . . . tock . . . tick . . . tock.* The inner workings of the exquisite timepiece clicked very slowly, but it seemed to be working.

"What a find!" Molly exclaimed, as she undid the old clasp and put the watch on her wrist. "I wonder if it will keep time."

Can you picture the watch? What words and phrases describe it?

cubbyhole: a small enclosed space

afghan: a knit or crocheted blanket or shawl

curlicue: with fancy twists and curls

Gently pulling out the winding stem, she set the watch to the time on her clock radio: 10:45. Then she pushed in the stem and rotated it between her finger and thumb for several more turns, being extra careful not to overwind it.

For a moment Molly sat there admiring her new watch, and then suddenly she realized that she'd forgotten all about her book report. If she didn't get busy, it would be midnight—or later—before she'd be done. She pulled the afghan over her shoulders and faced her computer screen.

Why is the cursor blinking so slowly? Molly thought. Then her attention was drawn to her window. The rain's furious drumming seemed to have slowed to an unhurried *splat . . . splat . . . splat.*

"That's odd," she muttered, looking at the sheets of water flowing down the pane. Then she heard her cat meowing and knew something was definitely wrong.

"*Meeeeeeee . . . oooowwwwww!*" the cat cried, sounding as if his voice box had been turned to a slower speed.

Molly stared at him. "Donald . . . what's wrong?"

The cat looked at her and meowed again. Molly shook her head to clear it. Donald's mouth was opening very slowly and it seemed like a year before any sound came out.

Why do you think everything has slowed down?

"I must be *really* sleepy," she told herself. "But I don't care how tired I am, I have to write this book report."

Determined, Molly put her hands on the keyboard and began to type, and suddenly the words seemed to come out easily. That didn't surprise her, though. After all, she'd liked the book, and she knew what she wanted to say about it. Now it was just a matter of sitting down and making herself do it.

Finally finished, she sat back and looked at what she'd written, amazed that she'd completed all three pages of the report so quickly. "Well, that was easy," she said with a satisfied smile. "I guess if I just set my mind to things and stop worrying about how late it's getting, I can do just about anything I want."

She looked at the beautiful watch on her wrist to see how long she'd taken to finish her report, and was disappointed to see that only five minutes had ticked by. "Darn, it must not work," she said. "There's no way I could have finished my paper in five minutes."

Slipping off the watch and putting it back in its box, Molly checked the digital clock radio by her bed. She rubbed her eyes and squinted. It couldn't be. The digits read 10:50. This was too weird. How could the watch and the clock radio both stop . . . at exactly the same time?

Molly opened the door and walked softly down the hall toward her parents' room. Her father's sawlike snoring echoed through the upstairs as she gently opened the door.

"Molly?" her mother called, sleepily.

"Sorry, Mom," Molly said. "I thought you'd be sound asleep by now. I just wanted to check your alarm clock since mine isn't—"

"Sound asleep?" her mother asked, sitting up. "I just left your room five minutes ago. Now come on, Molly. Get busy on that book report or you'll be up all night."

Molly walked back to her room with her heart thumping. Something was *very* weird. She walked over to the computer. Had she dreamed of writing her book report? No, there it was on the screen—all three pages of it.

"Okay, just calm down, girl," Molly told herself, lifting the watch out of the box and putting it on her wrist again. "There is an explanation for this. There has to be."

"*Meeeeeeeeeee . . . oooooowwwwwwww,*" Donald cried again, even more drawn out.

Molly watched her cat's mouth open and close in slow motion. No, it was moving slower than slow motion. She bent down and picked Donald up to carry him downstairs. Tiptoeing down the hallway, she heard the sawing sound of her father snoring. The sound of one intake of breath seemed to last all the way down the winding staircase to the landing of the basement stairs. What was going on?

Coming back up into the kitchen after putting Donald in his sleeping area, Molly decided that fixing herself a little snack before turning in might help calm her nerves. Walking into the pantry, she took out some crackers and peanut butter and poured herself a small glass of milk from the refrigerator. "I'm just a little overtired," she told herself as she munched on her snack. She chuckled to herself, "Either that or I'm going crazy." Then, starting to feel sleepy, she put everything away and headed back up to her room to turn in.

But the minute she laid eyes on her clock radio, she had to stifle a scream. It now read 10:51! She quickly looked at the watch on her wrist. Its metal hand had moved only a minute as well. "This is impossible!" she gasped, holding the watch up to her ear.

Tick . . . . . . tock . . . . . . tick . . . . . . tock.

Molly ran to the window.

Splat . . . . . . splat . . . . . . splat . . . . . . splat.

stifle: stop; hold back

It was totally unbelievable. She could hear each individual tick and tock of her watch, and she could see every single raindrop hitting the pane, bursting apart in a slow-motion spray, and flowing down the glass as sluggishly as honey.

Although she wanted to run in and tell her parents, Molly decided it was best just to go to bed. And so, after taking off her watch and setting it back in its box, she climbed into bed. "In the morning this will all be a dream," she told herself, pulling the covers over her head.

The next morning Molly was awakened by the sound of clumping feet racing down the hall. She was just sitting up and shaking her head, trying to clear the cobwebs of sleep, when she heard a car horn, then the sound of a door slamming. Groggily she realized that the sounds meant Steve was leaving for school.

School! Molly looked at her clock radio and felt a surge of panic. It was already 7:30! With all the strangeness that happened the night before, she'd forgotten to set her alarm, and now she had only fifteen minutes to eat, dress, and make it to the bus stop.

Her heart pumping wildly, Molly jumped out of bed and threw on her bathrobe. As she tied the belt, her eyes fell on the wooden box containing her watch.

"The kids at school will love this," she muttered to herself. With no time to shower, she quickly opened the box, lifted the watch off its little cushion, and slipped the beautiful timepiece onto her wrist.

And that's when it happened.

PREDICT

Is it a dream? What will happen when Molly wakes up in the morning? What details make you think as you do?

As soon as she latched the clasp of the watch, she heard the front door opening—*very* slowly. Then she heard the *clump . . . clump . . . clump* sound of footsteps on the stairs, only now there seemed to be an eternity between each footfall. Molly figured that Steve had forgotten something, and her idea was confirmed when she heard the long, drawn-out blare of a car horn echoing through the gray, drizzly morning.

But it wasn't until she walked to her window and saw Steve heading back to the car that everything came together in Molly's mind. Steve's legs were making the motions of running, but he was moving so slowly that it almost looked like . . . he was standing still.

That was it!

As she watched her brother running but getting practically nowhere, Molly suddenly saw the connection between her action of putting on the watch and everything slowing down. *It's as if everything is actually "winding" down,* she thought, smiling, as she now took all the time she wanted getting dressed. In fact, she did all of her preparations for school at a leisurely pace—everything except take a shower. She didn't know if the watch was waterproof and she didn't dare take it off.

"I've got all the time in the world," she snickered, <u>ambling</u> into the kitchen, then over to the basement door to let Donald in. "With my trusty new watch, even waiting until the last minute means I have more time than I need."

When he finally came into the kitchen, running in slow motion up the basement stairs, Donald stared up at

ambling: walking slowly

Molly and opened his mouth. *Meeeeeeee-owwwwww*, came the drawn-out sound from the hungry cat.

"This is so cool!" Molly exclaimed. Then she fed her cat, ate a bowl of cereal, made a sandwich for her lunch, and headed back upstairs to finish getting ready for school. When she had her backpack strapped on and was all set to head off, she looked over at her clock radio and grinned. It was only 7:35.

"No need to hurry," she said, checking her special watch—the polished black hands pointing out the same time. And with that, she <u>sauntered</u> back downstairs and out the front door.

Heading for the bus stop, Molly marveled at her good fortune, and as she got closer to the corner, she saw all the kids she rode with already there. They were goofing around as usual, splashing water on one another by stamping their feet in puddles.

But today, as Molly knew it would be, was very different. And sure enough, just as she'd suspected, as she walked up to them, Molly saw that the kids were all moving in slow motion, raising their sneakered feet inch by inch, their legs falling like feathers into the giant puddles, sending trails of water droplets up into the air and cascading down.

"Awesome," she muttered, as she saw each drop separately rising from beneath the stomping feet and flying through the air. "My watch doesn't tell time, it *controls* it!"

sauntered: walked very slowly and casually

Feeling powerful, knowing that with this knowledge she could just about change the course of her life, Molly carefully took the watch off and slipped it into the pocket of her raincoat.

No need to make time drag now, she thought. *I'll save my watch's power for times when I really need to slow things down.*

A month later, after much experimentation with her amazing watch, Molly pretty much had its power under control. Every morning she'd give herself all the time in the world to get ready for school, and whenever she had a test, she'd slow time down to a crawl so she had plenty of time to figure out all the answers.

But as much as Molly's amazing watch could control time, it couldn't control the nasty weather. That's why one late October night she found herself unable to fall asleep because of a terrible cold she'd gotten from being constantly exposed to the dampness.

Ahh-choo! Molly's sneeze echoed around her room. It was nearly midnight, and she had hardly slept a wink. She felt horrible and was sure this was the worst cold she'd ever had. Her throat felt like someone had dragged barbed wire through it, her head felt completely stuffed with cotton, her cough sounded like an Alaskan husky's bark, and she was tired to the bone.

Although she'd spent the past three days in bed, she still wasn't feeling any better. The only thing that wasn't bothering her was the fact that she was missing school. Ordinarily, she would have worried about making up her

PREDICT

Molly got her wish. How will her life change?

missed homework or tests. But now that she had the watch, that wasn't a problem anymore. She could be sick for a whole year, and Molly knew that she'd still have plenty of time to catch up.

In fact, because of her amazing watch, Molly had aced every test in the past month. Mr. Rand and her other teachers couldn't get over the difference in her work. They praised her time-management skills and used her as an example to other kids who were falling behind.

"Take Molly, here," one teacher said, putting his arm around her with pride as if somehow he was responsible for her sudden change in attitude and good grades. "She knows how to use every minute of her time."

Actually, the teacher was totally right. Molly now completed her tests with time enough to spare so that she could double-check all of her answers. She handed assignments in on time, if not early, and she was always sitting at her desk a full ten minutes before class started.

In spite of how lousy she felt, Molly had to smile whenever she thought about how easy it had been to transform herself from a struggling C student into an A student who found school a breeze.

"And it's all because of you," she whispered to her precious watch, lying on her nightstand. She hadn't worn it or wound it since she'd been sick in bed, but the hands pointed to one minute past midnight—the same time reflecting on her clock radio.

Quickly reaching for a tissue to catch a sudden sneeze, Molly blew her nose. *If only my watch could make this cold go away,* she thought, as she sneezed again and again.

And then a wonderful idea struck her.

The only way she was going to get better was if she got some real rest. But she was coughing and sneezing so much that all she was getting each night was a few minutes of sleep at a time. With the watch, however, she knew that each one of those minutes could seem like hours. Yes, by wearing her watch she could create the time she needed to heal!

Without another moment's hesitation, Molly reached over and carefully lifted the magnificent timepiece off her nightstand, marveling at how its silver and jade band shone in the dim yellow moonlight. Then she fastened it around her wrist.

Ahhhhhhhhhhhhhh-chooooooooooooo.

Molly smiled, knowing the watch was at work. Then she blew her nose, turned off the light and lay straight back on the pillow. She'd never felt so tired, but at least now she knew she was going to get all the rest she needed.

Molly's idea sounds like a good one. What could possibly go wrong?

The sound of low, throaty voices coming from outside her room drifted into Molly's brain. Through half-opened eyes she looked up at the ceiling. The gray light of morning seeped into the room.

I can't believe I slept all night, she thought. Then she glanced slowly down at the watch on her left wrist, the hands still pointed to midnight.

For a moment, Molly had an uncomfortable feeling as she remembered that she hadn't wound the watch in several days, then she shrugged it off and started to sit up.

But even though her brain commanded her body to move, Molly remained flat on her back.

That's strange, she thought, trying to lift her arm. But it didn't move either.

As if in a dream, Molly heard the door open, each creak lasting for what seemed an eternity. She tried to move her head to see who was entering the room, but it remained where it was, and she was forced to continue staring straight up at the ceiling through her half-opened eyes. It felt as if she had been lying like this for hours. Then, finally, Molly saw her parents and a woman wearing a <u>stethoscope</u> around her neck standing over her. Their voices were <u>guttural</u>, like a tape played at slow speed, and as she listened closely and figured out what they were saying, Molly's heart froze.

"She wasn't breathing when I checked on her, doctor," her father said slowly, choking back sobs. "I think she died in her sleep."

"She had a terrible cold," her mother added. "And when I came in to feel her forehead, I realized she had no pulse." Then, obviously overcome with grief, Molly's mother collapsed into her husband's arms.

Molly felt the cold stethoscope against her chest. Then she saw the doctor frown. And that was the last thing Molly saw. For the next thing the doctor did was bend over and, with the palm of her hand, cover Molly's face and gently close her eyelids.

Noooooooo! Molly's mind screamed as she tried to open her eyes and, at the same moment, realized that the time between willing her eyes to open and actually opening them

PREDICT

Will Molly get out of this predicament? Why or why not?

stethoscope: a medical device used to listen to the heart and lungs

guttural: harsh; formed deep in the throat

could be hours—just like the time between breaths . . . and heartbeats. Yes, time, Molly now understood, was endless for her now. For the watch on her wrist had obviously stopped, and each millisecond was a whole universe of time.

"I'm afraid there is nothing I can do," the doctor said. "I'll call the funeral home."

It could have been years later or it could have been a few moments when Molly felt her body being lifted from her bed. She could hear low, throaty sounds of sobbing in the chilly air, but she couldn't see anything. Though she'd commanded her brain to open her eyes long before, it could be weeks before her eyelids responded. Wanting to scream out that she was alive, Molly now knew it was useless. In fact, it might take months for her mouth to open and sound to come out.

From a distance, Molly could hear her mother's hysterical sobs and a man, whom Molly determined to be the funeral home director, saying something about picking out a favorite outfit.

"Yes, we'll bury her in overalls and a flannel shirt," her mother said.

"Oh, and we'll just leave that watch on her wrist," her father added, breaking down into tears. "Molly had certainly become fond of it lately."

Last Minute

▼ Learning from the Story

"Last Minute" has many references to clocks, watches, and time. Can you weave a detail through a story that well? Pick a subject, such as flying or pyramids. Work with several classmates to tell a group story about that subject. One person starts the story. As soon as he mentions the chosen subject, he can stop. The next person picks up where the previous storyteller left off. She can stop as soon as she refers to the chosen subject. Continue until everyone has contributed or the story ends, whichever comes first!

▼ Putting It into Practice

Have you woven important details throughout your comic book? For example, you might picture an object in the background early in your story. That object could become very important later in the story. You could also use a clever phrase or a play on words that casually mentions this object. Even your title can help hold your story together. Read over your comic book script. Tighten up the story by weaving in a few important details.

THIRTY STORIES

The writer stood and stretched his legs. Sitting at this desk for too long gave him a cramp, and it was time to move. He picked a baby carrot out of the cellophane bag and munched it as he moved to the floor-to-ceiling windows of his penthouse apartment.

He smiled slightly as he gazed out over the nightscape. From this height, the city looked like a blanket of lights spread out below him. It was beautiful. He'd worked long and hard to get here. He'd written screenplays, TV shows, articles, just about anything. But the project that brought him to this height was the book of scary short stories he'd written.

The book had become a huge bestseller. Kids all over the country, he heard, were too scared to go to sleep. In truth, some of the stories were so scary that even *he* had trouble reading them.

As he stretched again, the writer heard a noise behind him. He turned and saw a young boy standing across the room.

penthouse: an apartment on the top floor of a tall building

screenplays: scripts written for movies

"Excuse me," said the boy, holding up the book of scary stories. "Are you the man who wrote this book?'

The writer raised an eyebrow. "In the flesh. And who might you be?" he asked. "More important, how did you get in here?"

"Did you write *all* the scary stories by yourself?" the boy asked timidly.

In spite of himself, the writer felt his chest puff out with pride. "Why, yes," he answered. "I did."

The boy took a step closer. "Well, I really wanted to talk to you."

The writer, though puzzled, couldn't help but smile. A fan, any fan, was always welcome.

"Did you really like them?" the writer asked.

"Like them?" the boy said. "They scared me to death."

The writer smiled again. "Good. I try."

But the writer was troubled by the boy's seriousness. He suddenly remembered that he didn't know who this kid was and started to get nervous.

"What's your name again?" the writer asked.

"My name doesn't matter," the boy said. "There are a lot of kids like me out there. Kids who are afraid to go to sleep, or take a shower, or even leave the house." The boy was almost upon the writer now. "I couldn't sleep for days after I read your book. I got real sick. I . . . well, when I said you scared me to death, I meant it."

The writer felt his skin crawl. He was sure his hair was standing on end . . . especially when the boy's face started changing.

What do you think the boy means? Has a story ever scared you to death?

"This is how I looked when I died," the ghastly boy said, his eyes suddenly <u>hollow</u>, his cheeks sunken, his lips pulled back in fear. "And this is how I look now!" the boy screeched.

The writer saw the boy's face rot away. Worms appeared behind the empty eye sockets. The hands that reached toward him were bones and decayed flesh.

The writer jumped backward and crashed through the tall window of his penthouse apartment. The last thing he saw was the grinning skull of his dead fan leaning out of the broken window, gazing down at him.

hollow: blank; empty-looking

The writer certainly dropped like a stone. Thirty stories is a long way to fall.

THIRTY STORIES

▼ Learning from the Story

Here are just a few reasons why "Thirty Stories" would make a great comic book.

- It uses dialogue to tell the story.
- It's written from a third-person point of view.
- The characters are interesting.
- You can visualize the setting.

The only thing the story could use is a stronger title. Work with a group of two or three classmates to suggest at least ten new titles. Then vote on the best one. Once you have a great title, sprinkle in a few references to it throughout the story.

▼ Putting It into Practice

The cover of a comic book is like a good title—it grabs the reader's attention. Some call it "bait" for the reader. Have you thought about the cover of your comic book? It should include your title. It should also picture explosive action or hint at something horrible just about to happen. However, you don't want to give away the ending of your story. Pick an action-packed scene that might make a great cover. Choose one that will make any reader want to pick up your book.